the miffy crochet book

First published in the UK in 2026 by
Search Press Limited
Wellwood, North Farm Road,
Tunbridge Wells, Kent TN2 3DR

1 2 3 4 5 6 7 8 9 10

First published in Dutch as
het grote nijntje haakboek

Pattern designs, Kimberley Zwaans
Illustrations crochet stitches, Antoinette van Schaik
Photography crochet, Roland J. Reinders
Cover design, Josephine van Bennekom
Interior design, Femke den Hertog
Published in Dutch for the first time by Uitgeverij Luitingh-Sijthoff B.V., 2024, Amsterdam

English translation from the original Dutch by Burravoe

ISBN: 978-1-80092-420-8
ebook ISBN: 978-1-80093-378-1

Bookmarked Hub
For further ideas and inspiration, and to join our free online community, visit www.bookmarkedhub.com

Publishers' notes
Metric measurements are used in this book; the imperial conversions are rounded to the nearest ¼in. Always use either metric or imperial measurements, not a combination of both.

US crochet terms are used throughout this book. For a US to UK conversion chart please refer to page 18 and the inside front flap.

The Publishers and author can accept no responsibility for any consequences arising from the information, advice or instructions given in this publication.

For errata, please visit our website (www.searchpress.com) or the Bookmarked Hub (www.bookmarkedhub.com).

GPSR information can be found at www.searchpress.com
Printed in China, TT052026

the miffy crochet book

friends • fun times • bedtime

kimberley zwaans
based on the work of dick bruna

SEARCH PRESS

contents

preface

Welcome to this book of crochet patterns inspired by Dick Bruna's timeless illustrations. I am proud and excited to ask you to come with me on this creative adventure: *the miffy crochet book*. This book is divided into three themes: friends, fun times and bedtime, and has patterns for Miffy, Melanie, bunting, a comfort blanket and more.

Whether you are a seasoned crocheter or just starting out, *the miffy crochet book* offers something for everyone. The patterns are thoughtfully designed to appeal both to beginners and experienced crocheters, with clear instructions, step-by-step guidance, and plenty of pictures to ensure success with each project. The patterns are written using US terms. If you prefer to use UK terminology, please see the conversions on page 18 and the inside flap.

Working on this special project was truly a pleasure for me. As a Miffy enthusiast and passionate crocheter, turning Dick Bruna's beloved illustrations into crochet patterns was a dream come true. I hope the love and dedication I've poured into each design is reflected in the crochet creations you'll find in this book.

Miffy is an icon we all grew up with, and I hope this book will not only serve as a source of creative inspiration but also take you on a nostalgic journey back to your own childhood memories. So grab your crochet hook and let's bring Miffy's magic to life together, stitch by stitch.

Have fun crocheting!

With warm greetings,
Kimberley Zwaans

yarn

Two types of yarn were used: Durable Cosy fine (a cotton/acrylic mix) and Durable Coral (a cotton yarn). Both yarns are produced according to the OEKO-TEX® Standard 100. This means that they have been tested for harmful substances and are therefore safe for humans and ecologically harmless.

Because the characters are crocheted using soft Durable Cosy fine, they are wonderfully cuddly. The yarn used in this book can be replaced with other yarn of a similar weight and composition, though please note the finished projects may vary slightly from those shown in the book depending on the yarn used.

The yarns were specially chosen to match the colours in Dick Bruna's books, which were not quite primary colours. We have used a warm orange yarn for Miffy's dress, which Dick referred to as red.

Durable Cosy fine is a versatile yarn that can be used in many projects. One ball weighs 1¾oz (50g), with 115yd (105m) per ball. It is made of 58 per cent cotton and 42 per cent acrylic, which makes the yarn both strong and soft to the touch. This yarn is great for crocheting soft toys and blankets.

These are the colours used in this book:

- Durable Cosy fine in 310 White
- Durable Cosy fine in 2194 Orange
- Durable Cosy fine in 2106 Peacock Blue
- Durable Cosy fine in 2152 Leaf Green
- Durable Cosy fine in 2180 Bright Yellow
- Durable Cosy fine in 2218 Hazelnut
- Durable Cosy fine in 325 Black

Durable Coral has been available for more than 30 years. The yarn is soft and perfect for crochet projects like baby items or home accessories. It is made of 100 per cent mercerized cotton. One ball weighs 1¾oz (50g), with 137yd (125m) per ball. The mini variant weighs ¾oz (20g), with 55yd (50m) per ball.

The following colours are used in this book:

- Durable Coral in 310 White
- Durable Coral in 2194 Orange
- Durable Coral in 2106 Peacock Blue
- Durable Coral in 2152 Leaf Green
- Durable Coral in 2180 Bright Yellow

For every project, you will need a darning needle to weave in your yarn ends and a pair of sharp scissors to trim your yarn, along with the specific tools and materials listed on the individual project pages. Some projects also require fibre filling for stuffing and black thread or embroidery cotton/floss for finishing details.

basic stitches

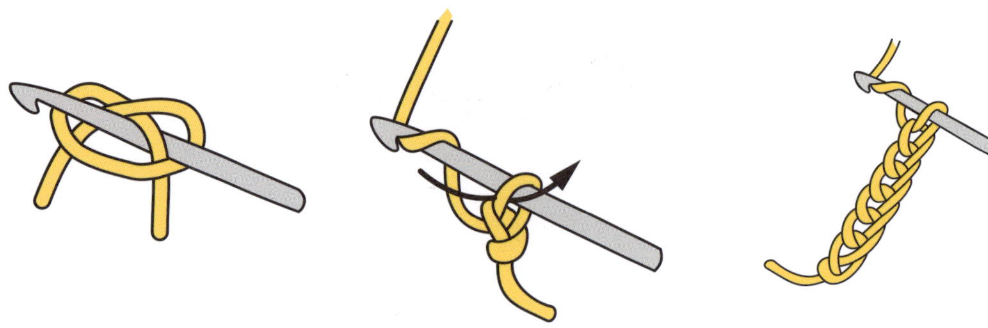

chain

Step 1: Make a slip knot and insert the hook through the loop.

Step 2: Wrap the yarn round the hook, then use the hook to pull a loop through the first loop.

Step 3: Repeat until you have a foundation chain of the desired length. This forms the foundation for all your work.

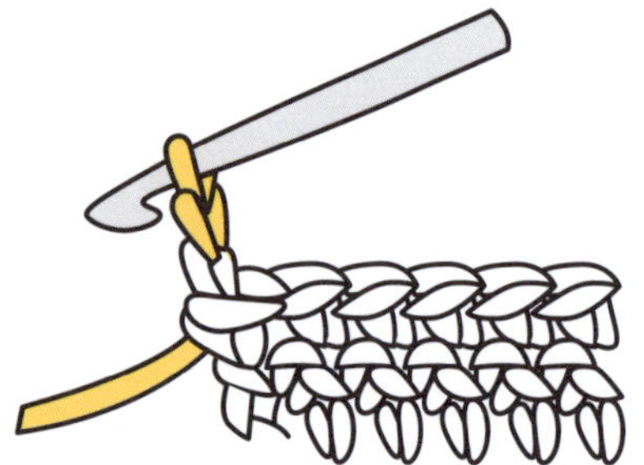

turning chain

Turning chains are worked in order to gain height.

single crochet = work 1 chain
half double crochet = work 2 chains
double crochet = work 3 chains
treble crochet = work 4 chains
double treble crochet = work 5 chains

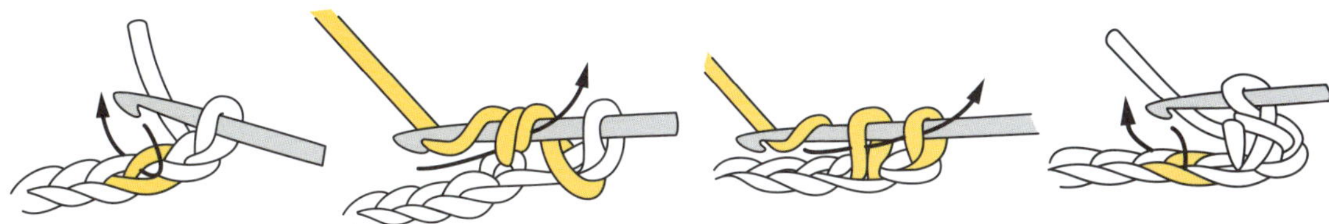

single crochet

Step 1: Once you have completed the foundation chain, start the first row by working single crochet stitches into it. You do this by inserting the crochet hook into the second foundation chain from the hook.

Step 2: Wrap the yarn round the hook and use the hook to pull the yarn through (pull up a loop).

Step 3: You now have 2 loops on the hook. Wrap the yarn round the hook again, then pull it through the 2 loops.

Step 4: This completes one single crochet stitch. To continue, insert the hook into the next foundation chain to make the next single crochet stitch.

Note: When starting a new row with single crochet, you work 1 turning chain.

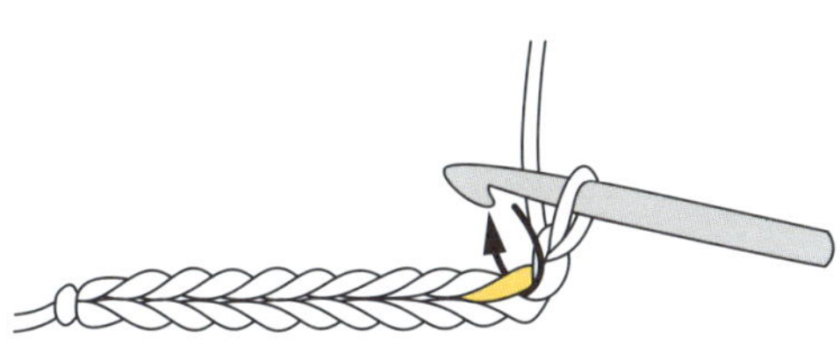

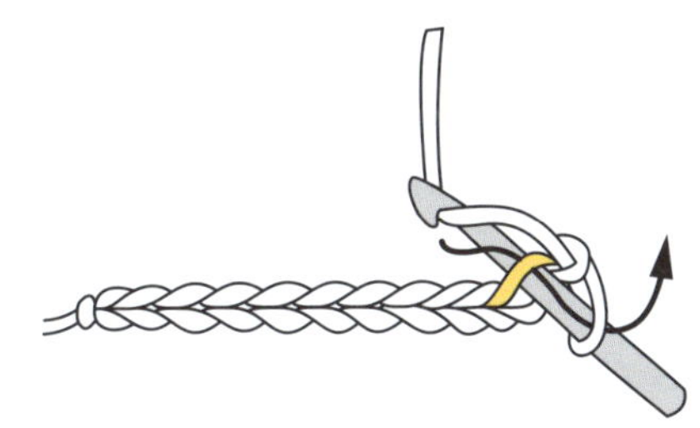

slip stitch

The slip stitch is the shortest crochet stitch. Insert the crochet hook into the foundation chain, yarn round, and pull the yarn through both the stitch and loop on your hook at the same time. This produces a flat stitch that is a bit tighter than the other stitches.

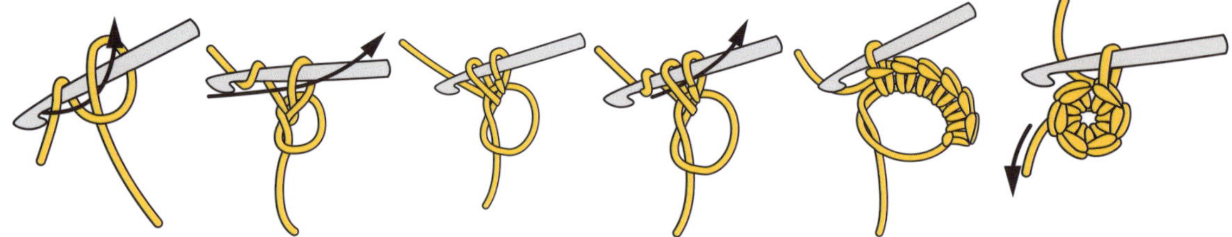

adjustable ring

Step 1: Form a wide loop by holding the yarn tail around your fingers and crossing the working yarn round it. Keep a firm grip on the crossover point, ensuring the working yarn stays behind the loop. Insert your hook through the wide loop and pull the working yarn through once.

Step 2: Yarn round hook and pull up a loop.

Step 3: Then work as many single crochet stitches as needed into the ring. Note, both the working yarn and the yarn tail form part of the ring.

Step 4: Gently pull the yarn tail to close the ring.

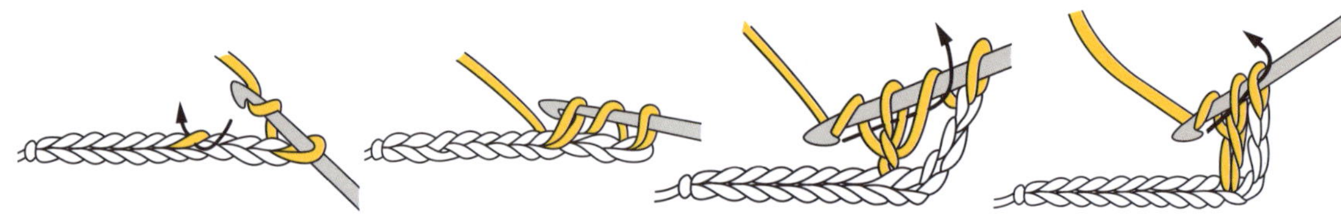

double crochet

Step 1: Wrap the yarn round your hook once. If starting from a foundation chain, skip 3 chains and insert your hook into the fourth chain from the hook. Wrap the yarn round the hook and pull up a loop.

Step 2: You now have 3 loops on your hook. Wrap the yarn round the hook again and pull it through the first 2 loops. You now have 2 loops remaining.

Step 3: Wrap the yarn round once more and pull through the remaining 2 loops to complete the stitch.

Note: When starting a new row with double crochet, make 3 turning chains.

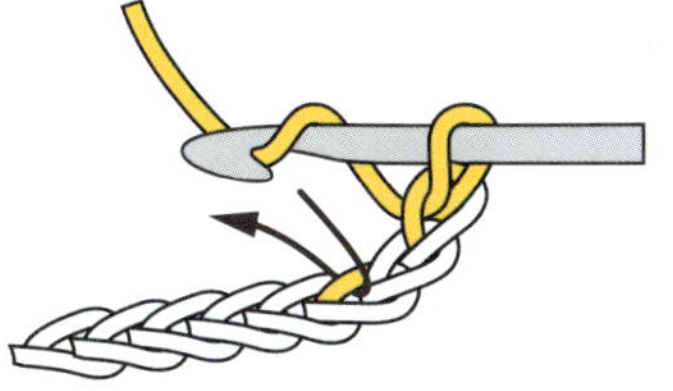
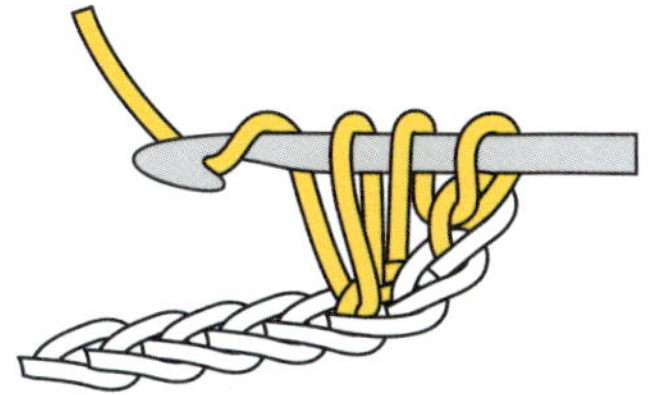

half double crochet

Step 1: Wrap the yarn round your hook once. If you are working from a chain, skip 2 chains and insert the hook into the third chain from the hook. Wrap the yarn round the hook and pull up a loop.

Step 2: You now have 3 loops on the hook. Wrap the yarn round again and pull it through all loops to complete the stitch.

Note: When starting a new row with half double crochet, you work 2 turning chains.

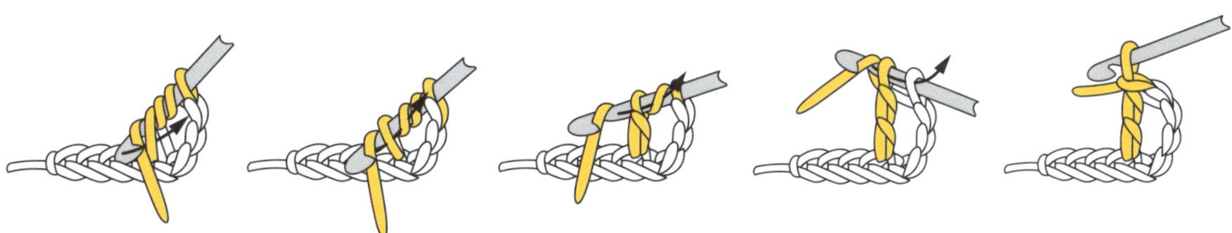

treble crochet

Step 1: Work 4 chains to get the height, yarn round twice, insert the hook into the fifth stitch/chain from the hook and yarn round. Pull up a loop.

Step 2: Yarn round and pull the yarn through the first 2 loops on the hook.

Step 3: Yarn round and pull the yarn through the next two loops.

Step 4: Yarn round and pull the yarn through the final 2 loops. This completes the treble crochet stitch.

Note: When starting a new row with treble crochet, work 4 turning chains.

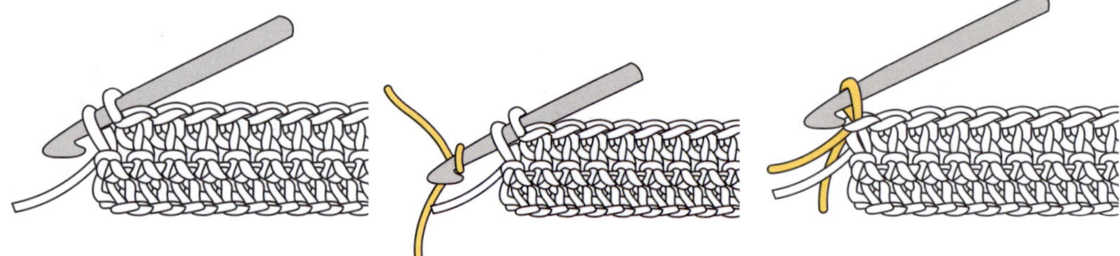

changing colours with single crochet

When you want to change colour, change the colour in the last yarn round of the current row. Insert the hook into the next loop and yarn round with the current colour and pull through a loop. Yarn round with the new colour and pull through both loops on hook. The next stitch now starts with the new colour.

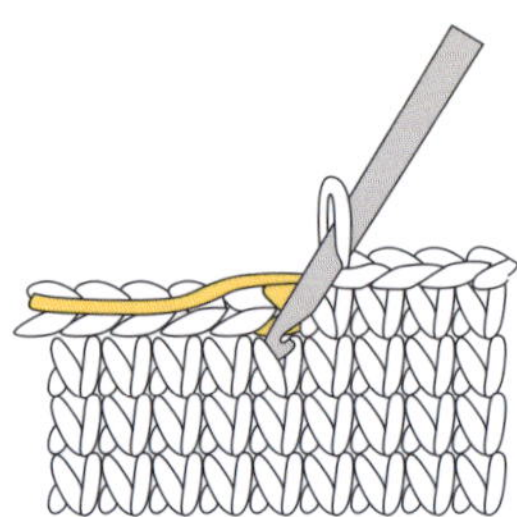

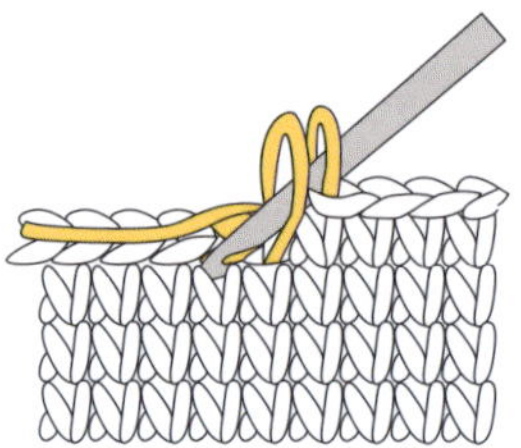

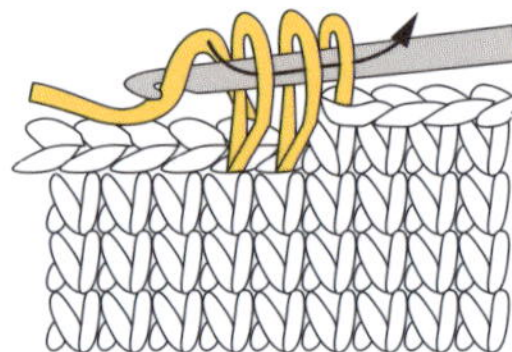

decreasing with single crochet

Step 1: Work 2 stitches together as follows: Insert the hook into the next stitch and pull the yarn through with your hook. You now have 2 loops on the crochet hook.

Step 2: Insert the hook into the next stitch and pull the yarn through again. You now have 3 loops on your crochet hook.

Step 3: Wrap the yarn round and pull the yarn through all the loops on the hook. You can see that you have now made 1 stitch where there were 2.

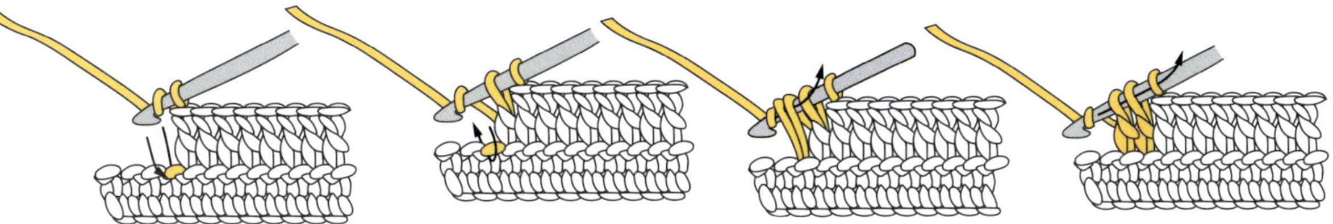

decreasing with double crochet

Step 1: Wrap the yarn round your hook once. Insert your hook into the next stitch and pull up a loop.

Step 2: You now have 3 loops on your hook. Wrap the yarn round the hook again and pull it through the first 2 loops. You now have 2 loops remaining on your hook.

Step 3: Repeat step 1.

Step 4: You now have 4 loops on your hook. Wrap the yarn round the hook again and pull it through the first 2 loops. You now have 3 loops remaining on your hook.

Step 5: Wrap the yarn round and pull through all loops on your hook. You can see that you have now made 1 double crochet stitch where there were 2.

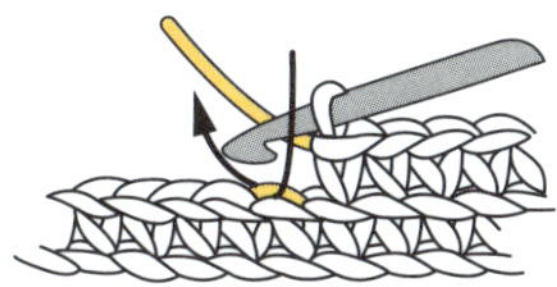

the back loop

Only insert your crochet hook into the back loop of each single crochet stitch from the previous row.

embroidering on your crochet work

There are many methods for embroidering eyes, noses and mouths. How you embroider depends entirely on what you are most comfortable with. Here is a brief explanation and some tips on how I like to embroider my projects. I always begin by counting my stitches to determine the exact placement for my embroidery, marking the spot with a pin. Then I thread my needle, secure the thread, and push the needle through from the back. I create a stitch by bringing the thread to the marked spot, then I begin embroidering by sewing around the stitch as I work. This also applies to a mouth: I bring the needle up on one side of the marked spot and guide the thread back down on the other side.

difficulty level

Easy

 Intermediate

 Difficult

US/UK equivalent crochet terms

US crochet terms are used in this book.
If you prefer to use UK terminology, please see the conversions below.

US	UK
sc single crochet	**dc** double crochet
hdc half double crochet	**htr** half treble crochet
dc double crochet	**tr** treble crochet
tr treble crochet	**dtr** double treble crochet
sc2tog sc 2 sts together	**dc2tog** dc 2 sts together
skip	**miss**

abbreviations

ar	adjustable ring
BL	back loop
ch	chain
FL	front loop
sl st	slip stitch
st(s)	stitch(es)
* *	asterisks mark a section of instructions to be repeated

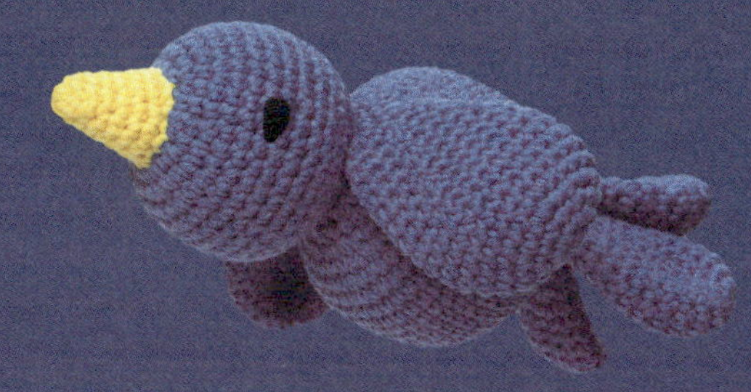

chapter 1
friends

Miffy

Miffy is the best-known character from Dick Bruna's books and, with this pattern, you can crochet her yourself. It is a straightforward pattern with almost no sewing; you only need to attach the arms to the body. Miffy's red dress is a separate pattern shown on page 30.

materials

2 balls of Durable Cosy fine yarn in 310 White; 1¾oz/50g/115yd/105m

3.5mm (US 4, UK 9/10) crochet hook

Fibre filling (for stuffing)

Black thread or embroidery cotton/floss

stitches

ar	adjustable ring
BL	back loop
ch	chain
FL	front loop
hdc	half double crochet
sc	single crochet
sc2tog	single crochet 2 stitches together

note

All parts of Miffy are worked in continuous rounds. Do not make a chain to start the next round, but simply continue crocheting. Use a stitch marker or a piece of yarn to mark the start of your round.

ears (make 2)

Round 1: 6 sc in an ar or work 2 ch and 6 sc in the second ch from hook (6 sts).

Round 2: 2 sc in each st (12 sts).

Round 3: 12 sc.

Round 4: *3 sc, 2 sc in next st*, repeat from * to * until the end of this round (15 sts).

Round 5: *4 sc, 2 sc in next st*, repeat from * to * until the end of this round (18 sts).

Rounds 6–14: 18 sc.

Round 15: *4 sc, sc2tog*, repeat from * to * until the end of this round (15 sts).

Rounds 16 and 17: 15 sc.

Fasten off and start crocheting the second ear. The second ear is not fastened off. Once you have completed the second ear, take the first ear and continue crocheting in the st after the last st in round 17 of the first ear.

With this round you will join the ears and begin working the head.

head

Round 1: 2 sc, 2 sc in next st, *4 sc, 2 sc in next st*, repeat from * to * across both ears and end with 2 sc (36 sts).
Round 2: *5 sc, 2 sc in next st*, repeat from * to * until the end of this round (42 sts).
Round 3: 7 sc, *1 sc, 2 sc in next st*, repeat from * to * twice more, 15 sc, *1 sc, 2 sc in next st*, repeat from * to * twice more, 8 sc (48 sts).
Rounds 4 and 5: 48 sc.
Round 6: 9 sc, *1 sc, 2 sc in next st*, repeat from * to * twice more, 18 sc, *1 sc, 2 sc in next st*, repeat from * to * twice more, 9 sc (54 sts).
Round 7: 54 sc.
Round 8: *8 sc, 2 sc in next st*, repeat from * to * until the end of this row (60 sts).
Rounds 9–15: 60 sc.
Round 16: *8 sc, sc2tog*, repeat from * to * until the end of this row (54 sts).
Round 17: 54 sc.
Round 18: *7 sc, sc2tog*, repeat from * to * until the end of this row (48 sts).
Round 19: 48 sc.
Round 20: *6 sc, sc2tog*, repeat from * to * until the end of this row (42 sts).
Round 21: 42 sc.

Stuff the ears and the head.

Round 22: *5 sc, sc2tog*, repeat from * to * until the end of this row (36 sts).
Round 23: *4 sc, sc2tog*, repeat from * to * until the end of this row (30 sts).
Round 24: *3 sc, sc2tog*, repeat from * to * until the end of this row (24 sts).

Now continue working in rounds for the start of the body.

body

Round 25: in the FL work *3 sc, 2 sc in next st*, repeat from * to * until the end of this row (30 sts).
Round 26: 2 sc, 2 sc in next st, *4 sc, 2 sc in next st*, repeat from * to * and end with 2 sc (36 sts).
Round 27: *5 sc, 2 sc in next st* repeat from * to * until the end of this row (42 sts).
Round 28: 3 sc, 2 sc in next st, *6 sc, 2 sc in next st*, repeat from * to * and end with 3 sc (48 sts).
Rounds 29 and 30: 48 sc.
Round 31: *7 sc, 2 sc in next st* repeat from * to * until the end of this row (54 sts).
Rounds 32–48: 54 sc.

Stuff the body while crocheting.

legs and feet

Now continue crocheting the legs and feet. To make the first leg:

Round 49: 9 sc, skip 27 sc, then work 18 sc until the end of this round (27 sts).
Rounds 50 and 51: 27 sc.
Round 52: *7 sc, sc2tog*, repeat from * to * until the end of this round (24 sts).
Round 53: 24 sc.
Round 54: *6 sc, sc2tog*, repeat from * to * until the end of this round (21 sts).
Round 55: 11 sc, in the FL work *1 hdc, 2 hdc in next st*, repeat from * to * twice more in the FL, 4 sc (24 sts).
Round 56: 11 sc, *2 sc, 2 sc in next st*, repeat from * to * twice more, 4 sc (27 sts).
Rounds 57 and 58: 27 sc.
Round 59: in the BL work *7 sc, sc2tog*, repeat from * to * until the end of this round (24 sts).
Round 60: *2 sc, sc2tog*, repeat from * to * until the end of this round (18 sts).

From here, continue stuffing the leg.

Round 61: *1 sc, sc2tog*, repeat from * to * until the end of this round (12 sts).
Round 62: *sc2tog*, repeat from * to * until the end of this round (6 sts).

Fasten off and close the ring.

For the second leg, rejoin the yarn to start at round 49.

Hold Miffy in front of you with the ears down and the finished leg on the right. Join the yarn at the back, skipping 3 sc and joining yarn in the fourth sc.

Rounds 49–51: 27 sc.
Round 52: *7 sc, sc2tog*, repeat from * to * until the end of this round (24 sts).
Round 53: 24 sc.
Round 54: *6 sc, sc2tog*, repeat from * to * until the end of this row (21 sts).
Round 55: 12 sc, in the FL work *1 hdc, 2 hdc in next st*, repeat from * to * twice more in the FL, 3 sc (24 sts).
Round 56: 12 sc, *2 sc, 2 sc in next st*, repeat from * to * twice more, 3 sc (27 sts).
Rounds 57 and 58: 27 sc.
Round 59: in the BL work *7 sc, sc2tog*, repeat from * to * until the end of this round (24 sts).
Round 60: *2 sc, sc2tog*, repeat from * to * until the end of this round (18 sts).

Stuff the leg.

Round 61: *1 sc, sc2tog*, repeat from * to * until the end of this round (12 sts).
Round 62: *sc2tog*, repeat from * to * until the end of this round (6 sts).

Fasten off and close the ring.

Opposite: Crocheting the arms.

arms (make 2)

Round 1: 6 sc in an ar or work 2 ch and 6 sc in the second ch from hook (6 sts).
Round 2: 2 sc in each st (12 sts).
Round 3: *3 sc, 2 sc in next st*, repeat from * to * until the end of this round (15 sts).
Round 4: *4 sc, 2 sc in next st*, repeat from * to * until the end of this round (18 sts).
Rounds 5–15: 18 sc.
Round 16: *4 sc, sc2tog*, repeat from * to * until the end of this round (15 sts).
Round 17: 15 sc.
Fasten off.

Make a second arm.

Stuff the lower part of the arm. Fold the arm flat and sew it in place on the body between rows 28 and 29. Embroider a cross for the mouth and ovals for the eyes using black thread or embroidery cotton/floss.

Embroider the eyes between rounds 14 and 16, spaced 9 stitches apart. Stitch the mouth between rounds 18 and 19 and rounds 20 and 21, making sure there are 4 stitches in between the points (see picture).

Miffy's dress

Miffy is characterized by her red dress. This is not difficult to crochet: the sleeves are two separate pieces and are sewn in place at the end. The dress closes at the back.

* materials

2 balls of Durable Cosy fine yarn in 2194 Orange; 1¾oz/50g/115yd/105m

3.5mm (US 4, UK 9/10) crochet hook

* stitches

ch	chain
FL	front loop
sc	single crochet
sl st	slip stitch

dress

The dress is worked in rows. Make 1 turning chain at the start of each row. This does not count as a stitch.

Work 37 ch.

Row 1: work 1 sc in the second ch from hook, 35 sc (36 sts). Turn.
Row 2: 1 ch, 3 sc, 2 sc in next st, *5 sc, 2 sc in next st*, repeat from * to * until you have 2 sts remaining, 2 sc (42 sts). Turn.
Row 3: 1 ch, 42 sc. Turn.
Row 4: 1 ch, *3 sc, 2 sc in next st*, repeat from * to * once more. 9 ch, then skip 6 sc, 2 sc in next st, 11 sc, 2 sc in next st, 9 ch, then skip 6 sc, 2 sc in next st, 3 sc, 2 sc in next st, 4 sc (54 sts). Turn.
Row 5: 1 ch, 54 sc, when working the chain spaces only work in the FL. Turn.
Row 6: 1 ch, 4 sc, 2 sc in next st, *8 sc, 2 sc in next st*, repeat from * to * until you have 4 sts remaining, 4 sc (60 sts). Turn.
Rows 7–27: 1 ch, 60 sc.
Fasten off.

Rejoin yarn to row 1 (the neck) and work a sl st in each st (36 sts).

sleeves (make 2)

The sleeves are worked in rows. Make 1 turning chain at the start of each row. This does not count as a stitch.

Work 21 ch.

Row 1: work 1 sc in the second ch from hook, 19 sc (20 sts). Turn.
Rows 2–10: 1 ch, 20 sc. Turn.
Row 11: 1 ch, sc2tog, 7 sc, sc2tog, 7 sc, sc2tog (17 sts).

Fasten off.

Make a second sleeve.

Sew the sleeve to the dress with a running stitch, then use the same stitch to sew the sleeve closed. Put the dress on Miffy and use running stitch to sew together the back of the dress.

1

2

3

4

5

Melanie

Melanie is Miffy's friend. Melanie's pattern consists largely of one piece: only the arms are sewn to the body later. Her yellow dress is a separate piece, included in this project.

* materials

2 balls of Durable Cosy fine yarn in 2218 Hazelnut (A), 3 balls in 2180 Bright Yellow (B); 1¾oz/50g/115yd/105m
3.5mm (US 4, UK 9/10) crochet hook
Fibre filling (for stuffing)
Black thread or embroidery cotton/floss

* stitches

ar	adjustable ring
BL	back loop
ch	chain
FL	front loop
hdc	half double crochet
sc	single crochet
sc2tog	single crochet 2 stitches together
sl st	slip stitch

* note

Melanie's ears, head, body, legs and arms are worked in continuous rounds. Do not make a chain to start the next round, but simply continue crocheting. Use a stitch marker or a piece of yarn to mark the start of your round.

ears (make 2)

Round 1: using yarn A, work 6 sc in an ar or work 2 ch and 6 sc in the second ch from hook (6 sts).
Round 2: 2 sc in each st (12 sts).
Round 3: 12 sc.
Round 4: *3 sc, 2 sc in next st*, repeat from * to * until the end of this round (15 sts).
Round 5: 15 sc.
Round 6: *4 sc, 2 sc in next st*, repeat from * to * until the end of this round (18 sts).
Rounds 7–14: 18 sc.
Round 15: *4 sc, sc2tog*, repeat from * to * until the end of this round (15 sts).
Rounds 16 and 17: 15 sc.

Fasten off and start working on the other ear. The second ear is not fastened off. Once you have crocheted the second ear, pick up the first ear.

With this round, the ears are joined together and the first round of the head is crocheted. Continue crocheting in the st after the last crocheted st of round 17 of the first ear. Now start round 1 of the head.

head

Round 1: 2 sc, 2 sc in next st, *4 sc, 2 sc in next st*, repeat from * to * across both ears and end with 2 sc (36 sts).
Round 2: *5 sc, 2 sc in next st*, repeat from * to * until the end of this row (42 sts).
Round 3: 7 sc, *1 sc, 2 sc in next st*, repeat from * to * twice more, 15 sc, *1 sc, 2 sc in next st*, repeat from * to * twice more, 8 sc (48 sts).
Round 4: 48 sc.
Round 5: 9 sc, *1 sc, 2 sc in next st*, repeat from * to * twice more, 18 sc, *1 sc, 2 sc in next st*, repeat from * to * twice more, 9 sc (54 sts).
Round 6: 54 sc.
Round 7: *8 sc, 2 sc in next st*, repeat from * to * until the end of this round (60 sts).
Rounds 8–15: 60 sc.
Round 16: *8 sc, sc2tog*, repeat from * to * until the end of this round (54 sts).
Round 17: 54 sc.
Round 18: *7 sc, sc2tog*, repeat from * to * until the end of this round (48 sts).
Round 19: 48 sc.
Round 20: *6 sc, sc2tog*, repeat from * to * until the end of this round (42 sts).
Round 21: 42 sc.

Stuff the ears and head.

Round 22: *5 sc, sc2tog*, repeat from * to * until end of round (36 sts).
Round 23: *4 sc, sc2tog*, repeat from * to * until the end of this round (30 sts).
Round 24: *3 sc, sc2tog*, repeat from * to * until the end of this round (24 sts).

body

Now continue crocheting. This is the start of the body.

Round 25: in the FL, work *3 sc, 2 sc in next st*, repeat from * to * until the end of this round (30 sts).
Round 26: 2 sc, 2 sc in next st, *4 sc, 2 sc in next st*, repeat from * to * and end with 2 sc (36 sts).
Round 27: *5 sc, 2 sc in next st*, repeat from * to * until the end of this round (42 sts).
Round 28: 42 sc.
Round 29: 3 sc, 2 sc in next st,*6 sc, 2 sc in next st*, repeat from * to * and end with 3 sc (48 sts).
Round 30: 48 sc.
Round 31: *7 sc, 2 sc in next st*, repeat from * to * until the end of this round (54 sts).
Rounds 32–48: 54 sc.

legs and feet

Now continue crocheting the legs and feet.

Round 49: 9 sc, then skip 27 sc and work 18 sc until the end of this round (27 sts).
Rounds 50 and 51: 27 sc.
Round 52: *7 sc, sc2tog*, repeat from * to * until the end of this round (24 sts).
Round 53: 24 sc.
Round 54: *6 sc, sc2tog*, repeat from * to * until the end of this round (21 sts).
Round 55: 11 sc, in the FL work *1 hdc, 2 hdc in next st*, repeat from * to * twice more, 4 sc (24 sts).
Round 56: 11 sc, *2 sc, 2 sc in next st*, repeat from * to * twice more, 4 sc (27 sts).
Rounds 57 and 58: 27 sc.
Round 59: in the BL work *7 sc, sc2tog*, repeat from * to * until the end of this round (24 sts).
Round 60: *2 sc, sc2tog*, repeat from * to * until the end of this round (18 sts). From here, stuff the body and the leg that has almost been fastened off.

Round 61: *1 sc, sc2tog*, repeat from * to * until the end of this round (12 sts).
Round 62: *sc2tog*, repeat from * to * until the end of the row (6 sts).

Fasten off and close the ring.

For the second leg, rejoin the yarn to round 49.

Hold Melanie with her ears facing down and the finished leg on the right-hand side.

Join yarn A at the back, skipping 3 sc and joining in the fourth sc.

Rounds 49–51: 27 sc.
Round 52: *7 sc, sc2tog*, repeat from * to * until the end of this round (24 sts).
Round 53: 24 sc.
Round 54: *6 sc, sc2tog*, repeat from * to * until the end of this row (21 sts).
Round 55: 12 sc, in the FL work *1 hdc, 2 hdc in next st*, repeat from * to * twice more, work 3 sc (24 sts).
Round 56: 12 sc, *2 sc, 2 sc in next st*, repeat from * to * twice more, 3 sc (27 sts).
Rounds 57 and 58: 27 sc.
Round 59: in the BL work *7 sc, sc2tog*, repeat from * to * until the end of this round (24 sts).
Round 60: *2 sc, sc2tog*, repeat from * to * until the end of this round (18 sts).

Stuff the leg.

Round 61: *1 sc, sc2tog*, repeat from * to * until the end of this round (12 sts).
Round 62: *sc2tog*, repeat from * to * until the end of this round (6 sts).

Fasten off and close the ring.

arms (make 2)

Round 1: using yarn A, work 6 sc in an ar or work 2 ch and 6 sc in the second ch from hook (6 sts).
Round 2: 2 sc in each st (12 sts).
Round 3: *3 sc, 2 sc in next st*, repeat from * to * until the end of this round (15 sts).
Round 4: *4 sc, 2 sc in next st*, repeat from * to * until the end of this round (18 sts).
Rounds 5–15: 18 sc.
Round 16: *4 sc, sc2tog*, repeat from * to * until the end of this round (15 sts).
Round 17: 15 sc.

Fasten off.

Make a second arm.

Stuff the lower part of the arm. Fold the arm flat and sew it in place on the body between rounds 28 and 29.

Embroider a cross as a mouth and ovals as eyes using black thread or embroidery cotton/floss. Embroider the eyes between rounds 14 and 16, spaced 9 stitches apart.

Create the mouth by making two diagonal stitches in an X shape between rounds 18 and 19 and rounds 20 and 21, making sure there is a space of 4 stitches in between the points (see photo).

dress

The dress is worked in rows. Make 1 turning chain at the start of each row. This does not count as a stitch.

Using yarn B, work 37 ch.

Row 1: work 1 sc in the second ch from hook, 35 sc (36 sts). Turn.
Row 2: 1 ch, 3 sc, 2 sc in next st, *5 sc, 2 sc in next st*, repeat from * to * until you have 2 sts remaining, 2 sc (42 sts). Turn.
Row 3: 1 ch, 42 sc. Turn.
Row 4: 1 ch, *3 sc, 2 sc in next st*, repeat from * to * once more, work 9 ch and skip 6 sc, 2 sc in next st, 11 sc, 2 sc in next st, work 9 ch and skip 6 sc, 2 sc in next st, 3 sc, 2 sc in next st, 4 sc (54 sts). Turn.
Row 5: 1 ch, 54 sc, in the chain spaces only the FLs. Turn.
Row 6: 1 ch, 4 sc, 2 sc in next st, *8 sc, 2 sc in next st*, repeat from * to * until you have 4 sts remaining, 4 sc (60 sts). Turn.
Rows 7–27: 1 ch, 60 sc.
Fasten off.

Rejoin yarn to row 1 (the neck) and work a sl st in each st (36 sts).

sleeves (make 2)

The sleeves are worked in rows. Make 1 turning chain at the start of each row. This does not count as a stitch.

Using yarn B, work 21 ch.

Row 1: work 1 sc in the second ch from hook, 19 sc (20 sts). Turn.
Rows 2–10: 1 ch, 20 sc. Turn.
Row 11: 1 ch, sc2tog, 7 sc, sc2tog, 7 sc, sc2tog (17 sts).

Fasten off.

Make a second sleeve.

Sew the sleeve to the dress with a running stitch, then use the same stitch to sew the sleeve closed. Put the dress on Melanie and use running stitch to sew up the back.

Poppy Pig

Poppy Pig is the aunt of Grunty, a friend of Miffy. Poppy Pig is a bit smaller than Miffy, but the pattern is designed in the same way, with separate arms. Poppy Pig wears a blue dress which is a separate piece, included in this project.

* materials

2 balls of Durable Cosy fine yarn in 2194 Orange (A) and 2106 Peacock Blue (B); 1¾oz/50g/115yd/105m
3.5mm (US 4, UK 9/10) crochet hook
Fibre filling (for stuffing)
Black thread or embroidery cotton/floss

* stitches

ar adjustable ring
BL back loop
ch chain
FL front loop
hdc half double crochet
sc single crochet
sc2tog single crochet 2 stitches together

* note

Poppy Pig's head, body, legs and ears are worked in continuous rounds. Do not make a chain to start the next round, but simply continue crocheting. Use a stitch marker or a piece of yarn to mark the start of your round.

head

Round 1: using yarn A, work 6 sc in an ar or work 2 ch and 6 sc in the second ch from hook (6 sts).
Round 2: 2 sc in each st (12 sts).
Round 3: *1 sc, 2 sc in next st*, repeat from * to * until the end of this round (18 sts).
Round 4: 1 sc, *2 sc in next st, 2 sc*, repeat from * to * until you have 2 sc remaining, 2 sc in next st, 1 sc (24 sts).
Round 5: *3 sc, 2 sc in next st*, repeat from * to * until the end of this round (30 sts).

Round 6: 2 sc, *2 sc in next st, 4 sc*, repeat from * to * until you have 3 sts remaining, 2 sc in next st, 2 sc (36 sts).
Round 7: 6 sc, *1 sc, 2 sc in next st*, repeat from * to * twice more, 12 sc, *1 sc, 2 sc in next st*, repeat from * to * twice more, 6 sc (42 sts).
Round 8: 42 sc.
Round 9: 8 sc, *1 sc, 2 sc in next st*, repeat from * to * twice more, 15 sc, *1 sc, 2 sc in next st*, repeat from * to * twice more, 7 sc (48 sts).
Rounds 10–13: 48 sc.
Round 14: 10 sc, *1 sc, 2 sc in next st*, repeat from * to * twice more, 17 sc, *1 sc, 2 sc in next st*, repeat from * to * twice more, 9 sc (54 sts).
Rounds 15–20: 54 sc.
Round 21: *7 sc, sc2tog*, repeat from * to * until the end of this round (48 sts).
Round 22: 48 sc.
Round 23: *6 sc, sc2tog*, repeat from * to * until the end of this round (42 sts).
Round 24: *5 sc, sc2tog*, repeat from * to * until the end of this round (36 sts).
Round 25: *4 sc, sc2tog*, repeat from * to * until the end of this round (30 sts).
Round 26: *3 sc, sc2tog*, repeat from * to * until the end of this round (24 sts).

body

We now continue crocheting in rounds for the start of the body.

Round 27: in the FL work *3 sc, 2 sc in next st*, repeat from * to * until the end of this row (30 sts).
Round 28: 2 sc, 2 sc in next st, *4 sc, 2 sc in next st*, repeat from * to * and end with 2 sc (36 sts).
Round 29: work *5 sc, 2 sc in next st*, repeat from * to * until the end of this round (42 sts).
Round 30: 3 sc, 2 sc in next st, *6 sc, 2 sc in next st*, repeat from * to * and end with 3 sc (48 sts).
Round 31: 48 sc.
Round 32: *7 sc, 2 sc in next st*, repeat from * to * until the end of this round (54 sts).
Round 33: 4 sc, 2 sc in next st, *8 sc, 2 sc in next st*, repeat from * to * and end with 4 sc (60 sts).
Rounds 34–46: 60 sc.
Round 47: 4 sc, sc2tog, *8 sc, sc2tog*, repeat from * to * and end with 4 sc (54 sts).

legs and feet

Now continue crocheting the legs and feet.

Round 48: 9 sc, skip 27 sc and work 18 sc until the end of this round (27 sts).
Rounds 49 and 50: 27 sc.
Round 51: *7 sc, sc2tog*, repeat from * to * until the end of this round (24 sts).
Round 52: *6 sc, sc2tog*, repeat from * to * until the end of this round (21 sts).
Round 53: 11 sc, in the FL work *1 hdc, 2 hdc in next st*, repeat from * to * twice more in the FL, 4 sc (24 sts).
Round 54: 11 sc, *2 sc, 2 sc in next st*, repeat from * to * twice more, 4 sc (27 sts).
Rounds 55 and 56: 27 sc.
Round 57: in the BL, work *7 sc, sc2tog*, repeat from * to * until the end of this round (24 sts).
Round 58: *2 sc, sc2tog*, repeat from * to * until the end of this round (18 sts).

From here, stuff the body and the leg that has almost been fastened off.

Round 59: *1 sc, sc2tog*, repeat from * to * until the end of this round (12 sts).
Round 60: *sc2tog*, repeat from * to * until the end of this round (6 sts).

Fasten off and close the ring.

For the second leg, rejoin the yarn to round 48.

Hold Poppy Pig with the head facing down, with the finished leg on the right-hand side. Join yarn A at the back, skipping 3 sc and joining in the fourth sc.

Rounds 48–50: 27 sc.
Round 51: *7 sc, sc2tog*, repeat from * to * until the end of this round (24 sts).
Round 52: *6 sc, sc2tog*, repeat from * to * until the end of this round (21 sts).
Round 53: 12 sc, in the FL work *1 hdc, 2 hdc in next st*, repeat from * to * twice more, 3 sc (24 sts).
Round 54: 12 sc, *2 sc, 2 sc in next st*, repeat from * to * twice more, 3 sc (27 sts).
Rounds 55 and 56: 27 sc.
Round 57: in the BL work *7 sc, sc2tog*, repeat from * to * until the end of this round (24 sts).
Round 58: *2 sc, sc2tog*, repeat from * to * until the end of this round (18 sts).

From here, continue stuffing the leg.

Round 59: *1 sc, sc2tog*, repeat from * to * until the end of this round (12 sts).
Round 60: sc2tog, repeat from * to * until the end of this round (6 sts).

Fasten off and close the ring.

ears (make 2)

Round 1: work 6 sc in an ar.
Round 2: *2 sc, 2 sc in next st*, repeat from * to * until the end of this round (8 sts).

Fasten off, leaving a long yarn tail for sewing in place. Fold the ears flat and sew them in place between rounds 6 and 9.

arms (make 2)

Round 1: using yarn A, 6 sc in an ar or work 2 ch and 6 sc in the second ch from hook (6 sts).
Round 2: 2 sc in each st (12 sts).
Round 3: *3 sc, 2 sc in next st*, repeat from * to * until the end of this round (15 sts).
Round 4: *4 sc, 2 sc in next st*, repeat from * to * until the end of this round (18 sts).
Rounds 5–14: 18 sc.
Round 15: *4 sc, sc2tog*, repeat from * to * until the end of this round (15 sts).
Round 16: 15 sc.

Fasten off.

Make a second arm.

Stuff the lower part of the arm.

Fold the arm flat and sew it in place on the body between rounds 29 and 30.

Embroider circles for the nose between rounds 16 and 19, embroider a mouth around rounds 20 and 21, and embroider ovals for the eyes on round 14 using black thread or embroidery cotton/floss.

dress

The dress is worked in rows. Make 1 turning chain at the start of each row. This does not count as a stitch.

Using yarn B, work 37 ch.

Row 1: 1 sc in the second ch from hook, 35 sc (36 sts). Turn.
Row 2: 1 ch, 3 sc, 2 sc in next st, *5 sc, 2 sc in next st*, repeat from * to * until you have 2 sts remaining, 2 sc (42 sts). Turn.
Row 3: 1 ch,*3 sc, 2 sc in next st*, repeat from * to * once more, work 9 ch and skip 6 sc, 2 sc in next st, 11 sc, 2 sc in next st, work 9 ch and skip 6 sc, 2 sc in next st, 3 sc, 2 sc in next st, 4 sc (54 sts). Turn.
Row 4: 1 ch, 54 sc, in the chain spaces only in the FL. Turn.
Row 5: 1 ch, 4 sc, 2 sc in next st, *8 sc, 2 sc in next st*, repeat from * to * until you have 4 sts remaining, 4 sc (60 sts). Turn.
Row 6: 1 ch, 60 sc.
Row 7: 1 ch, 4 sc, 2 sc in next st, *9 sc, 2 sc in next st*, repeat from * to * until you have 5 sts remaining, 5 sc (66 sts).
Rows 8–25: 66 sc.

Fasten off.

Rejoin yarn to row 1 (the neck) and work a sl st in each st (36 sts).

sleeves (make 2)

The sleeves are worked in rows. Make 1 turning chain at the start of each row. This does not count as a stitch.

Using yarn B, work 21 ch.

Row 1: work 1 sc in the second ch from hook, 19 sc (20 sts). Turn.
Rows 2–10: 1 ch, 20 sc. Turn.
Row 11: 1 ch, sc2tog, 7 sc, sc2tog, 7 sc, sc2tog (17 sts).

Fasten off.

Make a second sleeve.

Sew the sleeve to the dress with a running stitch, then use the same stitch to sew the sleeve closed. Put the dress on Poppy Pig and use running stitch to sew up the back.

Snuffy

Snuffy is a brave, sweet little dog with whom Miffy has all kinds of adventures. This crochet pattern is slightly more challenging as you have to sew the pieces together after crocheting them. It is advisable to pin all the pieces together securely, before sewing them in place.

materials

2 balls of Durable Cosy fine yarn in 2218 Hazelnut; 1¾oz/50g/115yd/105m
3.5mm (US 4, UK 9/10) crochet hook
Fibre filling (for stuffing)
Black thread or embroidery cotton/floss

stitches

ar	adjustable ring
ch	chain
hdc	half double crochet
sc	single crochet
sc2tog	single crochet 2 stitches together

note

All parts of Snuffy are worked in continuous rounds. Do not make a chain to start the next round, but simply continue crocheting. Use a stitch marker or a piece of yarn to mark the start of your round.

legs (make 4)

Round 1: work 6 sc in an ar or work 2 ch and 6 sc in the second ch from hook (6 sts).
Round 2: 2 sc in each st (12 sts).
Round 3: 12 sc.
Round 4: *1 sc, 2 sc in next st*, repeat from * to * until the end of this round (18 sts).
Rounds 5–9: 18 sc.
Round 10: *2 sc, 2 sc in next st*, repeat from * to * until the end of this round (24 sts).
Round 11: 6 sc, 6 hdc, 12 sc (24 sts).

Fasten off, leaving a long yarn tail to attach the legs.

Make sure to attach the legs with the hdc at the top, to allow the stitches to follow the curve.

Stuff the legs when sewing them in place.

body

Round 1: 6 sc in an ar or work 2 ch and 6 sc in the second ch from hook (6 sts).
Round 2: 2 sc in each st (12 sts).
Round 3: 1 sc, *2 sc in next st*, repeat from * to * twice more, 3 sc, *2 sc in next st*, repeat from * to * twice more, 2 sc (18 sts).
Round 4: 3 sc, *2 sc in next st*, repeat from * to * twice more, 6 sc, *2 sc in next st*, repeat from * to * twice more, 3 sc (24 sts).
Round 5: 5 sc, *2 sc in next st*, repeat from * to * twice more, 9 sc, *2 sc in next st*, repeat from * to * twice more, 4 sc (30 sts).
Round 6: 2 sc, *2 sc in next st, 4 sc*, repeat from * to * until you have 3 sts remaining, 2 sc in next st, 2 sc (36 sts).
Round 7: *5 sc, 2 sc in next st*, repeat from * to * until the end of this round (42 sts).
Rounds 8–24: 42 sc.
Round 25: *5 sc, sc2tog*, repeat from * to * until the end of this round (36 sts).
Round 26: 2 sc, *sc2tog, 4 sc*, repeat from * to * until you have 4 sts remaining, sc2tog, 2 sc (30 sts).
Round 27: 8 sc, *sc2tog*, repeat from * to * twice more, 9 sc, *sc2tog*, repeat from * to * twice more, 1 sc (24 sts).
Round 28: 6 sc, *sc2tog*, repeat from * to * twice more, 6 sc, *sc2tog*, repeat from * to * twice more (18 sts).

Stuff the body.

Round 29: *1 sc, sc2tog*, repeat from * to * until the end of this round (12 sts).
Round 30: *sc2tog*, repeat from * to * until the end of this round (6 sts).

Fasten off and close the ring.

tail

Round 1: work 6 sc in an ar or work 2 ch and 6 sc in the second ch from hook (6 sts).
Round 2: 2 sc in each st (12 sts).
Rounds 3–6: 12 sc.

Fasten off, leaving a substantially long yarn tail to sew the tail in place at the back.

Stuff the tail while sewing it in place.

head

Round 1: 6 sc in an ar or work 2 ch and 6 sc in the second ch from hook (6 sts).
Round 2: 2 sc in each st (12 sts).
Round 3: *1 sc, 2 sc in next st*, repeat from * to * until the end of this round (18 sts).
Round 4: 3 sc, *2 sc in next st*, repeat from * to * twice more, 6 sc, *2 sc in next st*, repeat from * to * twice more, 3 sc (24 sts).
Round 5: 5 sc, *2 sc in next st*, repeat from * to * twice more, 9 sc, *2 sc in next st*, repeat from * to * twice more, 4 sc (30 sts).
Round 6: 2 sc, *2 sc in next st, 4 sc*, repeat from * to * until you have 3 sc remaining, 2 sc in next st, 2 sc (36 sts).
Round 7: 36 sc.
Round 8: *5 sc, 2 sc in next st*, repeat from * to * until the end of this round (42 sts).
Round 9: 8 sc, *1 sc, 2 sc in next st*, repeat from * to * twice more, 15 sc, *1 sc, 2 sc in next st*, repeat from * to * twice more, 7 sc (48 sts).
Rounds 10–18: 48 sc.
Round 19: 10 sc, *1 sc, sc2tog*, repeat from * to * twice more, 15 sc, *1 sc, sc2tog*, repeat from * to * twice more, 5 sc (42 sts).
Round 20: *5 sc, sc2tog*, repeat from * to * until the end of this round (36 sts).
Round 21: 2 sc, *sc2tog, 4 sc*, repeat from * to * until you have 4 sts remaining, sc2tog, 2 sc (30 sts).
Round 22: 7 sc, *sc2tog*, repeat from * to * twice more, 9 sc, *sc2tog*, repeat from * to * twice more, 2 sc (24 sts).
Round 23: 5 sc, *sc2tog*, repeat from * to * twice more, 6 sc, *sc2tog*, repeat from * to * twice more, 1 sc (18 sts).

Stuff the head, fasten off and sew it in place on the body between rounds 5 and 6 and rounds 10 and 11.

ears (make 2)

Round 1: 6 sc in an ar or work 2 ch in the second ch from hook 6 sc.
Round 2: 2 sc in each st (12 sts).
Round 3: 1 sc, *2 sc in next st*, repeat from * to * twice more, 3 sc, *2 sc in next st*, repeat from * to * twice more, 2 sc (18 sts).
Rounds 4–11: 18 sc.
Round 12: *1 sc, sc2tog*, repeat from * to * until the end of this round (12 sts).
Round 13: *sc2tog*, repeat from * to * until the end of this round (6 sts).

Fasten off. To attach the ears, lay each one at a diagonal angle onto the head, between rounds 5 and 7. Stitch in place at the top to secure. The tip of each ear should point towards the face.

Using black thread or embroidery cotton/floss, embroider eyes on round 13 at 7 stitch intervals, and a nose between rounds 14 and 15. Create a mouth by embroidering from the snout to round 16.

bird

The pattern for the bird consists of several pieces and, as with Snuffy, it is advisable to pin the pieces securely, before sewing them in place.

* materials

2 balls of Durable Cosy fine yarn in 2106 Peacock Blue (A), 1 ball in 2180 Bright Yellow (B); 1¾oz/50g/115yd/105m
3.5mm (US 4, UK 9/10) crochet hook
Fibre filling (for stuffing)
Black thread or embroidery cotton/floss

* stitches

ar	adjustable ring
sc	single crochet
sc2tog	single crochet 2 stitches together

* note

All parts of the bird are worked in continuous rounds. Do not make a chain to start the next round, but simply continue crocheting. Use a stitch marker or a piece of yarn to mark the start of your round.

body

Round 1: using yarn A, work 6 sc in an ar.
Round 2: 2 sc in each st (12 sts).
Round 3: *1 sc, 2 sc in next st*, repeat from * to * until the end of this round (18 sts).
Round 4: 1 sc, *2 sc in next st, 2 sc*, repeat from * to * until you have 2 sts remaining, 2 sc in next st, 1 sc (24 sts).
Round 5: *3 sc, 2 sc in next st*, repeat from * to * until the end of this round (30 sts).

Round 6: 2 sc, *2 sc in next st, 4 sc*, repeat from * to * until you have 3 sts remaining, 2 sc in next st, 2 sc (36 sts).
Round 7: *5 sc, 2 sc in next st*, repeat from * to * until the end of this round (42 sts).
Rounds 8–16: 42 sc.
Stuff the body.
Round 17: *5 sc, sc2tog*, repeat from * to * until the end of this round (36 sts).
Round 18: 2 sc, *sc2tog, 4 sc*, repeat from * to * until you have 4 sts remaining, sc2tog, 2 sc (30 sts).
Round 19: *3 sc, sc2tog*, repeat from * to * until the end of this round (24 sts).
Round 20: 1 sc, *sc2tog, 2 sc*, repeat from * to * until you have 3 sts remaining, sc2tog, 1 sc (18 sts).
Round 21: *1 sc, sc2tog*, repeat from * to * until the end of this round (12 sts).

Ensure the body is fully stuffed.

Round 22: *sc2tog*, repeat from * to * until the end of this round (6 sts).

Close the ring and fasten off.

head

Round 1: using yarn A, 6 sc in an ar.
Round 2: 2 sc in each st (12 sts).
Round 3: *1 sc, 2 sc in next st* repeat from * to * until the end of this round (18 sts).
Round 4: 1 sc, *2 sc in next st, 2 sc*, repeat from * to * until you have 2 sts remaining, 2 sc in next st, 1 sc (24 sts).
Round 5: *3 sc, 2 sc in next st*, repeat from * to * until the end of this round (30 sts).
Round 6: 2 sc, *2 sc in next st, 4 sc*, repeat from * to * until you have 3 sts remaining, 2 sc in next st, 2 sc (36 sts).
Rounds 7–13: 36 sc.
Stuff the head.

Round 14: 2 sc, *sc2tog, 4 sc*, repeat from * to * until you have 4 sts remaining, sc2tog, 2 sc (30 sts).
Round 15: *3 sc, sc2tog*, repeat from * to * until the end of this round (24 sts).
Round 16: 1 sc, *sc2tog, 2 sc*, repeat from * to * until you have 3 sts remaining, sc2tog, 1 sc (18 sts).

Fasten off, leaving a long yarn tail, stuff the head and sew in place on the body (using the photographs for help with positioning).

wings (make 2)

Round 1: using yarn A, 6 sc in an ar.
Round 2: 2 sc in each st (12 sts).
Round 3: *1 sc, 2 sc in next st*, repeat from * to * until the end of this round (18 sts).
Round 4: 1 sc, *2 sc in next st, 2 sc*, repeat from * to * until you have 2 sts remaining, 2 sc in next st, 1 sc (24 sts).
Rounds 5–9: 24 sc.
Round 10: *6 sc, sc2tog*, repeat from * to * until the end of this round (21 sts).
Round 11: 21 sc.
Round 12: *5 sc, sc2tog*, repeat from * to * until the end of this round (18 sts).
Round 13: 18 sc.
Round 14: *4 sc, sc2tog*, repeat from * to * until the end of this round (15 sts).
Round 15: 15 sc.
Round 16: *3 sc, sc2tog*, repeat from * to * until the end of this round (12 sts).
Round 17: 12 sc.
Round 18: *sc2tog*, repeat from * to * until the end of this round (6 sts).

Fasten off and sew in place on the sides of the neck (between head and body pieces), slightly below halfway (see pictures for placement).

tail feathers (make 3)

Round 1: using yarn A, 6 sc in an ar.
Round 2: 2 sc in each st (12 sts).
Round 3: 1 sc, *2 sc in next st*, repeat from * to * twice more, 3 sc, *2 sc in next st*, repeat from * to * twice more, 2 sc (18 sts).
Rounds 4–6: 18 sc.
Round 7: *4 sc, sc2tog*, repeat from * to * until the end of this round (15 sts).
Rounds 8 and 9: 15 sc.
Round 10: *3 sc, sc2tog*, repeat from * to * until the end of this round (12 sts).
Rounds 11 and 12: 12 sc.
Round 13: *sc2tog*, repeat from * to * until the end of this round (6 sts).

Fasten off and sew the tail feathers in place on the back between rounds 3 and 4.

beak

Row 1: using yarn B, 6 sc in an ar.
Row 2: 6 sc.
Row 3: *1 sc, 2 sc in next st*, repeat from * to * until the end of this round (9 sts).
Row 4: 9 sc.
Row 5: *2 sc, 2 sc in next st*, repeat from * to * until the end of this round (12 sts).
Row 6: 12 sc.
Row 7: *3 sc, 2 sc in next st*, repeat from * to * until the end of this round (15 sts).

Fasten off, stuff and sew the beak in place on the head between rounds 3 and 4. Embroider the eyes with black thread or embroidery cotton/floss between rounds 9 and 10, on both the right and left sides.

chapter 2
fun times

birthday cake

A cake is a must for a birthday party! This is an adorable table decoration and the advantage is that you can use this Miffy cake for lots of different parties. The number of candles can be adjusted as desired!

* materials

2 balls of Durable Coral yarn in 2194 Orange (A), 1 ball in 2180 Bright Yellow (B), 310 White (C), 2106 Peacock Blue (D) and 2152 Leaf Green (E); 1¾oz/50g/137yd/125m
2.5mm (US 1/2, UK 12/13) crochet hook
Corrugated cardboard
Fibre filling (for stuffing)
Black thread

* stitches

ar	adjustable ring
BL	back loop
dc	double crochet
FL	front loop
hdc	half double crochet
sc	single crochet
sl st	slip stitch
tr	treble crochet

* note

All parts of the birthday cake are worked in continuous rounds. Do not make a chain to start the next round, but simply continue crocheting. Use a stitch marker or a piece of yarn to mark the start of your round.

cake board (make 2)

Round 1: using yarn A, work 6 sc into an ar.

Round 2: 2 sc in each st (12 sts).

Round 3: *1 sc, 2 sc in next st* repeat from * to * until the end of this round (18 sts).

Round 4: 1 sc, 2 sc in next st, *2 sc, 2 sc in next st*, repeat from * to * until you have 1 st remaining, 1 sc (24 sts).

Round 5: *3 sc, 2 sc in next st*, repeat from * to * until the end of this round (30 sts).

Round 6: 2 sc, 2 sc in next st, *4 sc, 2 sc in next st*, repeat from * to * until you have 2 sts remaining, 2 sc (36 sts).

Round 7: *5 sc, 2 sc in next st*, repeat from * to * until the end of this round (42 sts).

Round 8: 3 sc, 2 sc in next st, *6 sc, 2 sc in next st*, repeat from * to * until you have 3 sts remaining, 3 sc (48 sts).

Round 9: *7 sc, 2 sc in next st*, repeat from * to * until the end of this round (54 sts).

Round 10: 4 sc, 2 sc in next st, *8 sc, 2 sc in next st*, repeat from * to * until you have 4 sts remaining, 4 sc (60 sts).

Round 11: *9 sc, 2 sc in next st*, repeat from * to * until the end of this round (66 sts).

Round 12: 5 sc, 2 sc in next st, *10 sc, 2 sc in next st*, repeat from * to * until you have 5 sts remaining, 5 sc (72 sts).

Round 13: *11 sc, 2 sc in next st*, repeat from * to * until the end of this round (78 sts).

Round 14: 6 sc, 2 sc in next st, *12 sc, 2 sc in next st*, repeat from * to * until you have 6 sts remaining, 6 sc (84 sts).

Round 15: *13 sc, 2 sc in next st*, repeat from * to * until the end of this round (90 sts).

Round 16: 7 sc, 2 sc in next st, *14 sc, 2 sc in next st*, repeat from * to * until you have 7 sts remaining, 7 sc (96 sts).

Round 17: *15 sc, 2 sc in next st*, repeat from * to * until the end of this round (102 sts).

Round 18: 8 sc, 2 sc in next st, *16 sc, 2 sc in next st*, repeat from * to * until you have 8 sts remaining, 8 sc (108 sts).

Round 19: *17 sc, 2 sc in next st*, repeat from * to * until the end of this round (114 sts).

Round 20: 9 sc, 2 sc in next st, *18 sc, 2 sc in next st*, repeat from * to * until you have 9 sts remaining, 9 sc (120 sts).

Round 21: *19 sc, 2 sc in next st*, repeat from * to * until the end of this round (126 sts).

Round 22: 10 sc, 2 sc in next st, *20 sc, 2 sc in next st*, repeat from * to * until you have 10 sts remaining, 10 sc (132 sts).

Round 23: *21 sc, 2 sc in next st*, repeat from * to * until the end of this round (138 sts).

Round 24: 11 sc, 2 sc in next st, *22 sc, 2 sc in next st*, repeat from * to * until you have 11 sts remaining, 11 sc (144 sts).

Round 25: *23 sc, 2 sc in next st*, repeat from * to * until the end of this round (150 sts).

Round 26: 12 sc, 2 sc in next st, *24 sc, 2 sc in next st*, repeat from * to * until you have 12 sts remaining, 12 sc (156 sts).
Round 27: *25 sc, 2 sc in next st*, repeat from * to * until the end of this round (162 sts).
Round 28: 13 sc, 2 sc in next st, *26 sc, 2 sc in next st*, repeat from * to * until you have 13 sts remaining, 13 sc (168 sts).
Round 29: *27 sc, 2 sc in next st*, repeat from * to * until the end of this round (174 sts).
Round 30: 14 sc, 2 sc in next st, *28 sc, 2 sc in next st*, repeat from * to * until you have 14 sts remaining, 14 sc (180 sts).

Fasten off and start working the second piece. Do not fasten off the second cake board.

Place the fastened-off part on a piece of cardboard and trace out a circle with a pencil, then cut out the circle.

Sandwich the cardboard between the two cake board pieces, so right sides are facing out. With yarn A still attached to second piece, work them together with 180 sc.

birthday cake

Round 1: using yarn C, work 6 sc into an ar.
Round 2: 2 sc in each st (12 sts).
Round 3: *1 sc, 2 sc in next st*, repeat from * to * until the end of this round (18 sts).
Round 4: 1 sc, 2 sc in next st, *2 sc, 2 sc in next st*, repeat from * to * until you have 1 st remaining, 1 sc (24 sts).
Round 5: *3 sc, 2 sc in next st*, repeat from * to * until the end of this round (30 sts).
Round 6: 2 sc, 2 sc in next st, *4 sc, 2 sc in next st*, repeat from * to * until you have 2 sts remaining, 2 sc (36 sts).
Round 7: *5 sc, 2 sc in next st*, repeat from * to * until the end of this round (42 sts).
Round 8: 3 sc, 2 sc in next st, *6 sc, 2 sc in next st*, repeat from * to * until you have 3 sts remaining, 3 sc (48 sts).
Round 9: *7 sc, 2 sc in next st*, repeat from * to * until the end of this round (54 sts).
Round 10: 4 sc, 2 sc in next st, *8 sc, 2 sc in next st*, repeat from * to * until you have 4 sts remaining, 4 sc (60 sts).
Round 11: *9 sc, 2 sc in next st*, repeat from * to * until the end of this round (66 sts).
Round 12: 5 sc, 2 sc in next st, *10 sc, 2 sc in next st*, repeat from * to * until you have 5 sts remaining, 5 sc (72 sts).
Round 13: *11 sc, 2 sc in next st*, repeat from * to * until the end of this round (78 sts).
Round 14: 6 sc, 2 sc in next st, *12 sc, 2 sc in next st*, repeat from * to * until you have 6 sts remaining, 6 sc (84 sts).
Round 15: *13 sc, 2 sc in next st*, repeat from * to * until the end of this round (90 sts).
Round 16: 7 sc, 2 sc in next st, *14 sc, 2 sc in next st*, repeat from * to * until you have 7 sts remaining, 7 sc (96 sts).
Round 17: *15 sc, 2 sc in next st*, repeat from * to * until the end of this round (102 sts).
Round 18: 8 sc, 2 sc in next st, *16 sc, 2 sc in next st*, repeat from * to * until you have 8 sts remaining, 8 sc (108 sts).
Round 19: *17 sc, 2 sc in next st*, repeat from * to * until the end of this round (114 sts).
Round 20: 9 sc, 2 sc in next st, *18 sc, 2 sc in next st*, repeat from * to * until you have 9 sts remaining, 9 sc (120 sts).
Round 21: in the BL work 120 sc.

Change to yarn B.

Rounds 22 and 23: 120 sc.
Round 24: *19 sc, 2 sc in next st*, repeat from * to * until the end of this round (126 sts).
Rounds 25–28: 126 sc.
Round 29: *20 sc, 2 sc in the next st*, repeat from * to * until the end of this round (132 sts).
Rounds 30 and 31: 132 sc.

Fasten off, leaving a long yarn tail to sew in place on the cake board.

Join in yarn C in the last FL of round 21, keeping the white part towards you as you crochet. This way, the stitches fall in the right direction.

Round 1: 1 ch, *1 sc, 2 hdc, 2 dc, 3 tr in next st, 2 dc, 2 hdc, 1 sc*, repeat from * to * to the end of this round until you have 11 arches (143 sts).
Round 2: *3 sl st, 2 sc, 2 hdc in each st, 2 sc, 3 sl st*, repeat from * to * until the end of this row (176 sts).

Fasten off, leaving a long yarn tail to sew the arches in place on the yellow part of the cake.

Place the white part of the cake onto a piece of cardboard and trace around the edge. Then, cut out the cardboard and place it inside the cake to reinforce it.

Now sew the cake in place on the cake board between rounds 22 and 23 of the cake board. Stuff the cake while you are sewing.

candles (make 5)

Crochet with yarns A, B, D and E.

Round 1: 6 sc into an ar.
Round 2: 2 sc in each st (12 sts).
Rounds 3–12: 12 sc.

Fasten off, leaving a long yarn tail.

flames (make 5)

Round 1: using yarn B, 2 sc, 2 hdc, 2 dc, 1 tr, 2 dc, 2 hdc, 2 sc into an ar (13 sts).

Fasten off and sew the flames to the candles using black thread. Pull the thread through the adjustable ring of the flame, then thread both ends through the adjustable ring of the candle. Tie a knot and pull it tight.

Stuff the candle, then sew it in place on the cake.

Tip: This cake features five candles, but you can customize the number and colours to match the birthday child's age and preference.

bunting

It's not a proper party without Miffy bunting! Crochet Miffy's silhouette in different colours and make bunting out of it later. Change the colours and the length of the bunting to fit your space or occasion.

✱ materials

1 ball of Durable Coral yarn in 2194 Orange (A), 2180 Bright Yellow (B), 310 White (C), 2106 Peacock Blue (D) and 2152 Leaf Green (E); 1¾oz/50g/137yd/125m

2.5mm (US 1/2, UK 12/13) crochet hook

✱ stitches

ch	chain
sc	single crochet
sc2tog	single crochet 2 stitches together
sl st	slip stitch

Tip: If the bunting curls up a bit, place a slightly damp tea towel on top, and gently smooth out. The bunting can be reinforced with fabric stiffener or sugar water if desired.

Using yarns A, B, C, D or E, work 21 ch.

Row 1: 1 sc in the second ch from hook, 19 sc (20 sts). Turn.
Row 2: 1 ch, 4 sc, sc2tog, *3 sc, sc2tog*, repeat from * to * once more, 4 sc (17 sts). Turn.
Row 3: 1 ch, 8 sc, sc2tog, 7 sc (16 sts). Turn.
Row 4: 1 ch, 16 sc. Turn.

Fasten off.

Count out 3 sc from the edge and rejoin the yarn. This will be row 5.

Row 5: 1 ch, 3 sc. Turn.
Row 6: 1 ch, 2 sc in the first st, 2 st (4 sts). Turn.
Row 7: 1 ch, 3 sc, 2 sc in the last st (5 sts).

Fasten off.

Count 4 sc along row 4 and rejoin the yarn. This becomes row 5 again.

Row 5: 1 ch, 3 sc. Turn.
Row 6: 1 ch, 2 sc, 2 sc in the last st (4 sts). Turn.
Row 7: 1 ch, 2 sc in the first st, 3 sc (5 sts).

Do not fasten off. Work 4 ch.

Row 8: 1 sc in the second ch from hook, 2 sc, 5 sc across the first leg, 5 sc across the second leg, 4 ch (16 sts). Turn.
Row 9: 1 sc in the second ch from hook, 15 sc (16 sts). Turn.
Rows 10 and 11: 16 sc. Turn.
Row 12: 1 ch, sc2tog, 12 sc, sc2tog (14 sts). Turn.
Row 13: 1 ch, sc2tog, 10 sc, sc2tog (12 sts). Turn.
Row 14: 1 ch, sc2tog, 8 sc, sc2tog (10 sts). Turn.
Row 15: 1 ch, sc2tog, 6 sc, sc2tog (8 sts). Turn.
Row 16: 1 ch, 2 sc in the first st, 6 sc, 2 sc in the last sc (10 sts). Turn.
Row 17: 1 ch, 2 sc in the first st, 8 st, 2 sc in the last st (12 sts). Turn.
Rows 18–20: 1 ch, 12 sc. Turn.
Row 21: 1 ch, sc2tog, 8 sc, sc2tog (10 sts). Turn.
Row 22: 1 ch, sc2tog, 6 sc, sc2tog (8 sts). Turn.
Row 23: 1 ch, 3 sc and leave the rest of the stitches unworked. Turn.
Row 24: 1 ch, 2 sc, 2 sc in next st (4 sts). Turn.
Rows 25–27: 1 ch, 4 sc. Turn.
Row 28: 1 ch, *sc2tog*, repeat from * to * once more (2 sts). Turn.
Row 29: 1 ch, 2 sc.

Fasten off and count 2 sc along row 22, join yarn there and work 3 sc. Turn. This is row 23.

Now work rows 24–29 on the left.

Row 24: 1 ch, 2 sc in the first sc, 2 sc (4 sts). Turn.
Rows 25–27: 1 ch, 4 sc. Turn.
Row 28: 1 ch, *sc2tog*, repeat from * to * once more (2 sts). Turn.
Row 29: 1 ch, 2 sc.

Do not fasten off. Work around the whole bunny. Sl st into each st and row end around, including between the legs. To join the bunnies to each other, sew them together at the arms and bases, stitching along the edge stitches. You could also thread a thin (transparent) wire through the ears so the bunnies don't bend forwards. This way, they can be hung up as a festive garland straightaway.

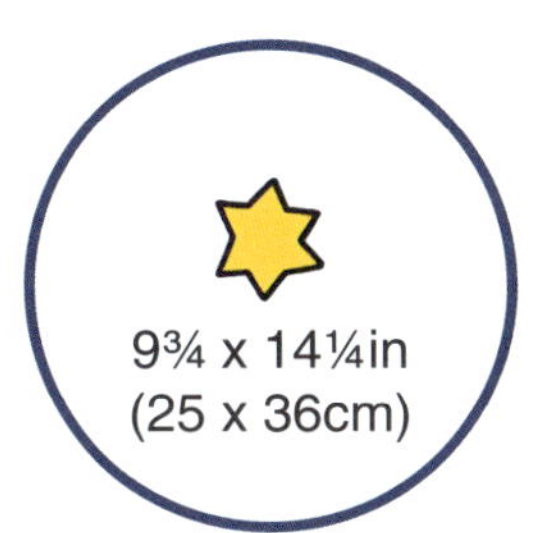

placemat

Combine this placemat with the coasters on page 80 and the party table is complete! The placemats consist of a single layer and have a coloured border. It's no problem if anything spills on them as they can easily be washed.

materials

2 balls of Durable Cosy fine yarn in 310 White (A); 1¾oz/50g/115yd/105m

For the border you will need:
1 ball of Durable Cosy fine yarn in 2194 Orange (B), 2180 Bright Yellow (C), 2106 Peacock Blue (D) and 2152 Leaf Green (E); 1¾oz/50g/115yd/105m
6mm (US 10, UK 4) crochet hook
Black thread or embroidery cotton/floss

stitches

ar	adjustable ring
ch	chain
dc	double crochet
hdc	half double crochet
sc	single crochet
sl st	slip stitch

Double-stranded crochet: use two strands of Durable Cosy fine, held together.

Round 1: using two strands of yarn A, 6 sc into an ar.
Round 2: 2 sc in each st (12 sts).
Round 3: *1 sc, 2 sc in next st* repeat from * to * until the end of this round (18 sts).
Round 4: 1 sc, *2 sc in next st, 2 sc*, repeat from * to * until you have 2 sts remaining, 2 sc in next st, 1 sc (24 sts).

Round 5: *3 sc, 2 sc in next st*, repeat from * to * until the end of this round (30 sts).
Round 6: 2 sc, *2 sc in next st, 4 sc*, repeat from * to * until you have 3 sts remaining, 2 sc in next st, 2 sc (36 sts).
Round 7: *5 sc, 2 sc in next st*, repeat from * to * until the end of this round (42 sts).
Round 8: 3 sc, *2 sc in next st, 6 sc*, repeat from * to * until you have 4 sts remaining, 2 sc in next st, 3 sc (48 sts).
Round 9: *7 sc, 2 sc in next st*, repeat from * to * until the end of this round (54 sts).
Round 10: 4 sc, *2 sc in next st, 8 sc*, repeat from * to * until you have 5 sts remaining, 2 sc in next st, 4 sc (60 sts).
Round 11: *9 sc, 2 sc in next st*, repeat from * to * until the end of this round (66 sts).
Round 12: 5 sc, *2 sc in next st, 10 sc*, repeat from * to * until you have 6 sts remaining, 2 sc in next st, 5 sc (72 sts).
Round 13: 12 sc, 17 ch, 1 sc into the second ch from hook, 15 sc, 1 sl st in the sc where the chain began, 11 sc, 17 ch, 1 sc in the second ch from hook, 15 sc, 1 sl st in the sc where the foundation chain began, *11 sc, 2 sc in next st*, repeat from * to * until you have 1 st remaining, 1 sc (110 sts).
Round 14: 12 sc, in the chains work 4 sc, 10 hdc, 2 sc, 2 sc in the first st, 15 sc, skip 1 sl st and 1 sc, 9 sc, skip 1 sc, then work in the chains 16 sc, 2 sc in the first st, 2 sc, 10 hdc, 3 sc, skip the sl st, *12 sc, 2 sc in next st*, repeat from * to * until you have 1 st remaining, 1 sc (144 sts).
Round 15: 12 sc, 2 hdc, 12 dc, 2 hdc, *2 hdc in next st*, repeat from * to * once more, 2 hdc, 13 dc, skip 2 sc, 5 sc, skip 2 sc, 14 dc, 2 hdc, *2 hdc in next st*, repeat from * to * once more, 2 hdc, 12 dc, 2 hdc, 12 sc, 2 sc in next st, *13 sc, 2 sc in next st*, repeat from * to * until you have 1 st remaining, 1 sc (148 sts).
Round 16: 12 sc, 16 hdc, *2 hdc in next st*, repeat from * to * three more times, 14 sc, skip 1 sc, then work 1 sl st, 4 sc, skip 1 sc, then work 1 sl st, 14 sc, *2 hdc in next st*, repeat from * to * three more times, 14 hdc, 62 sc (154 sts).

Fasten off and weave in the yarn end.

Embroider the eyes between rounds 9 and 10, and the mouth between rounds 10 and 13, spacing about 4 sc apart.

border

Using a single strand of yarn B, C, D or E, work 154 sl st around the edge.

Tip: If you need to clean the placemat, put it in a laundry bag and wash it on a hand-wash cycle at 86°F/30°C. If the placemat curls a little after washing, place a slightly damp tea towel over it and gently smooth it out.

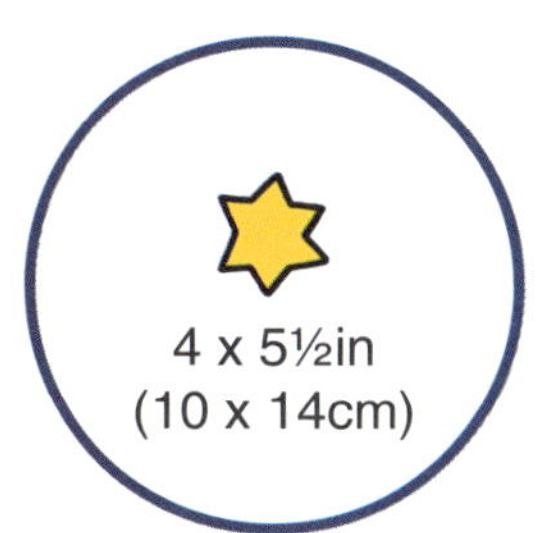

coasters

These coasters are ideal for children's parties.
The coasters consist of two layers, super cute and ready in no time.
Each coaster has a border in a different colour, creating a cheerful overall look.

materials

1 ball of Durable Cosy fine yarn in 310 White (for two coasters) (A); 1¾oz/50g/115yd/105m

For the border, you will need leftover yarn in the following colours:
Durable Coral yarn in 2194 Orange (B), 2180 Bright Yellow (C), 2106 Peacock Blue (D) and 2152 Leaf Green (E); 1¾oz/50g/137yd/125m
3.5mm (US 4, UK 9/10) crochet hook
Black thread or embroidery cotton/floss

stitches

ar adjustable ring
ch chain
hdc half double crochet
sc single crochet
sl st slip stitch

note

The coasters are worked in continuous rounds. Do not make a chain to start the next round, but simply continue crocheting. Use a stitch marker or a piece of yarn to mark the start of your round.

Tip: To clean the coasters, wash them on a hand-wash cycle at 86°F/30°C, placing the coasters in a laundry bag.

If the coasters curl a little after washing, place a slightly damp tea towel over them and gently smooth them out.

coasters (make 2)

Round 1: using yarn A, work 6 sc into an ar.

Round 2: 2 sc in each st (12 sts).

Round 3: *1 sc, 2 sc in next st* repeat from * to * until the end of this round (18 sts).

Round 4: 1 sc, *2 sc in next st, 2 sc*, repeat from * to * until you have 2 sts remaining, 2 sc in next st, 1 sc (24 sts).

Round 5: *3 sc, 2 sc in next st*, repeat from * to * until the end of this round (30 sts).

Round 6: 2 sc, *2 sc in next st, 4 sc*, repeat from * to * until you have 3 sts remaining, 2 sc in next st, 2 sc (36 sts).

Round 7: *5 sc, 2 sc in next st*, repeat from * to * until the end of this round (42 sts).

Round 8: 7 sc, 11 ch, then work 1 sc in the second ch from hook, 9 sc, 1 sl st in the sc where the chain began, 6 sc, 11 ch, then 1 sc in the second ch from hook, 9 sc, 1 sl st in the sc where the chain began, *6 sc, 2 sc in next st*, repeat from * to * until the end of this round, 1 sc (68 sts).

Round 9: 7 sc, work 2 sc in the chain, 6 hdc, 2 sc, 2 sc in the first st, 9 sc, skip the sl st and 1 sc, 4 sc, skip 1 sc, then work 10 sc in the chain, 2 sc in the first sc, 2 sc, 6 hdc, 1 sc, skip the sl st, *7 sc, 2 sc in next st*, repeat from * to * until you have 1 st remaining, 1 sc (90 sts).

Round 10: 9 sc, 6 hdc, 2 sc, *2 sc in next st*, repeat from * to * once more, 2 sc, 6 hdc, 1 sc, skip 1 sc, then work 3 sc, skip 1 sc, then work 1 sc, 6 hdc, 2 sc, *2 sc in next st*, repeat from * to * once more, 2 sc, 6 hdc, 12 sc, 2 sc in next st, *7 sc, 2 sc in next st*, repeat from * to * once more, 9 sc (95 sts).

Embroider the eyes with black thread or embroidery cotton/floss between rounds 6 and 7, as well as the mouth. As the eyes are positioned higher in the round, leave a space of about 4 sc between the eye and the mouth on round 6.

Make another coaster but do not embroider a face. Put the coasters on top of each other, right sides out and crochet together in round 11.

Round 11: join yarn B, C, D or E, work the two pieces together with 95 sl st in the last round.

festive crown

Whoever wears the crown is the birthday boy or girl, or give the crown to the prince or princess of the day. The crown is adjustable and designed for children between 1 and 5 years old – ideal for a family or even a school class. The adjustable closure is made with a hook and loop fastening.

* materials

1 ball of Durable Cosy fine yarn in 2180 Bright Yellow; 1¾oz/50g/115yd/105m
3mm (US 2/3, UK 11) crochet hook
Hook and loop fastening
Sewing needle
Sewing thread
Scissors

* stitches

ch	chain
sc	single crochet
sl st	slip stitch

Tip: If you find it difficult to sew on the hook and loop fastening, you can glue it in place with fabric glue instead.

crown

The crown is worked in rows. Make 1 turning chain at the start of each row. This does not count as a stitch.

Row 1: 1 sc in the second ch from hook, 109 sc (110 sts). Turn.
Rows 2–8: 1 ch, 110 sc. Turn.

You now have a long strip, measuring 21¾–23½in (55–60cm).

points of the crown

Row 9: 10 sc and leave the rest of the stitches unworked (10 sts). Turn.
Row 10: 1 ch, skip 1 sc, 9 sc (9 sts). Turn.
Row 11: 1 ch, skip 1 sc, 8 sc (8 sts). Turn.
Row 12: 1 ch, skip 1 sc, 7 sc (7 sts). Turn.
Row 13: 1 ch, skip 1 sc, 6 sc (6 sts). Turn.
Row 14: 1 ch, skip 1 sc, 5 sc (5 sts). Turn.
Row 15: 1 ch, skip 1 sc, 4 sc (4 sts). Turn.
Row 16: 1 ch, skip 1 sc, 3 sc (3 sts). Turn.
Row 17: 1 ch, skip 1 sc, 2 sc (2 sts). Turn.
Row 18: 1 ch, skip 1 sc, 1 sc (1 st).

This is the first point of the crown; fasten off. Join yarn, not in the first sc next to the first point but into the second sc.

Repeat rows 9–18 until you have 10 points. Fasten off the yarn and rejoin it to sl st around the entire piece.

hook and loop fastening

Now, attach a strip of hook and loop fastening about 1½in (4cm) long on the inside and three pieces of hook and loop fastening, each ¾in (2cm) long, on the outside, with a ¾in (2cm) gap between them.

chapter 3
bedtime

baby mobile

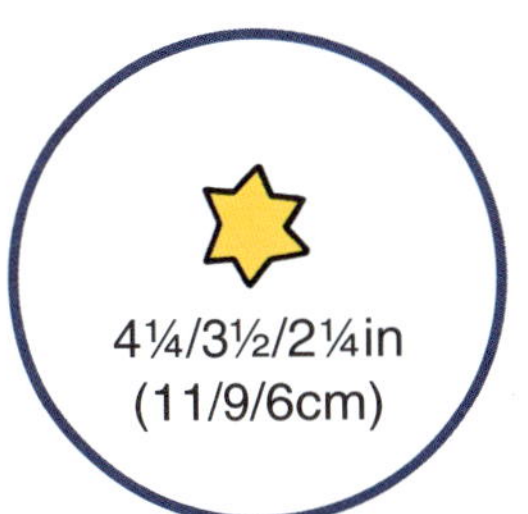

Brighten up your baby's room with this colourful mobile featuring a moon surrounded by stars. You could hang it above your baby's playpen, where your little one will be enchanted by its playful colours and gentle movement. The six-pointed stars come in two sizes, and you can adjust the number of stars to shape the mobile just the way you like.

★ materials

1 ball of Durable Coral yarn in 2180 Bright Yellow (A), 2106 Peacock Blue (B), 2194 Orange (C) and 2152 Leaf Green (D); 1¾oz/50g/137yd/125m
2.5mm (US 1/2, UK 12/13) crochet hook
Fibre filling (for stuffing)
Wax cord
6in (15cm) wooden ring
¾in (18mm) wooden beads x 10

★ stitches

ar	adjustable ring
ch	chain
sc	single crochet
sl st	slip stitch

★ note

The moon and stars (except the points) are worked in continuous rounds. Do not make a chain to start the next round, but simply continue crocheting. Use a stitch marker or a piece of yarn to mark the start of your round.

moon

Round 1: using yarn A, work 8 sc into an ar, or work 2 ch, then work 8 sc into the second chain from hook (8 sts).
Round 2: 2 sc in each st (16 sts).
Round 3: *1 sc, 2 sc in next st* repeat from * to * until the end of this round (24 sts).
Round 4: *1 sc, 2 sc in next st* repeat from * to * until the end of this round (36 sts).
Round 5: *(2 sc in next st) twice, 4 sc, 2 sc in next st, 4 sc, 2 sc in next st, 4 sc, (2 sc in next st) twice*, repeat from * to * once more (48 sts).

Round 6: (2 sc in next st) twice, 20 sc, *2 sc in next st*, repeat from * to * three more times, 20 sc, *2 sc in next st*, repeat from * to * once more (56 sts).
Round 7: (2 sc in next st) twice, 24 sc, *2 sc in next st*, repeat from * to * three more times, 24 sc, *2 sc in next st*, repeat from * to * once more (64 sts).
Round 8: *(2 sc in next st) twice, 9 sc, 2 sc in next st, 8 sc, 2 sc in next st, 9 sc, (2 sc in next st) twice*, repeat from * to * once more (76 sts).
Round 9: (2 sc in next st) twice, 34 sc, *2 sc in next st*, repeat from * to * three more times, 34 sc, *2 sc in next st*, repeat from * to * once more (84 sts).
Round 10: *(2 sc in next st) three times, 8 sc, 2 sc in next st, 8 sc, 2 sc in next st, 9 sc, 2 sc in next st, 8 sc, (2 sc in next st) three times*, repeat from * to * once more (102 sts).
Round 11: 102 sc.
Round 12: *(2 sc in next st) twice, 12 sc, 2 sc in next st, 10 sc, 2 sc in next st, 10 sc, 2 sc in next st, 12 sc, (2 sc in next st) twice*, repeat from * to * once more (116 sts).
Round 13: 116 sc.

Cut a length of wax cord and tie a double knot in it. Fold the moon in half and crochet together with sl st, lightly stuffing and inserting the cord as you go (58 sts).

large stars (make 3)

Round 1: using yarn A, C or D, 6 sc into an ar, or work 2 ch, then work 6 sc into the second chain from hook (6 sts).

Round 2: 2 sc in each st (12 sts).
Round 3: *1 sc, 2 sc in next st* repeat from * to * until the end of this round (18 sts).
Round 4: *2 sc, 2 sc in next st*, repeat from * to * until the end of this round (24 sts).
Round 5: *3 sc, 2 sc in next st*, repeat from * to * until the end of this round (30 sts).
Round 6: *4 sc, 2 sc in next st*, repeat from * to * until the end of this round (36 sts).
Row 7: work 6 sc, 1 ch (6 sts). Turn.
Row 8: skip 1 sc, work 5 sc, 1 ch (5 sts). Turn.
Row 9: skip 1 sc, work 4 sc, 1 ch (4 sts). Turn.
Row 10: skip 1 sc, work 3 sc, 1 ch (3 sts). Turn.
Row 11: skip 1 sc, work 2 sc, 1 ch (2 sts). Turn.
Row 12: skip 1 sc, then work 1 sc (1 st).

This is the first point. Fasten off and rejoin the yarn in the st next to the first point. Repeat rows 7–12 until you have 6 points.

Work a second star and then work the two pieces together as below. Cut a piece of wax cord and tie a double knot in it. Place the two stars wrong sides together and begin crocheting them together, working 1 sc in each st and 3 sc in each point. Lightly stuff and insert the cord as you work.

Cut the cords different lengths so each star hangs at a different height.

small stars (make 4)

Round 1: using yarn A, B, C or D, 6 sc into an adjustable ring, or work 2 ch, then work 6 sc into the second chain from hook (6 sts).
Round 2: 2 sc in each st (12 sts).
Round 3: *1 sc, 2 sc in next st* repeat from * to * until the end of this round (18 sts).
Round 4: *2 sc, 2 sc in next st*, repeat from * to * until the end of this round (24 sts).
Row 5: work 4 sc, 1 ch (4 sts). Turn.
Row 6: skip 1 sc, work 3 sc, 1 ch (3 sts). Turn.
Row 7: skip 1 sc, work 2 sc, 1 ch (2 sts). Turn.
Row 8: skip 1 sc, work 1 sc (1 st).

This is the first point; fasten off and join yarn in the sc next to the first point. Repeat rows 5–8 until you have 6 points.

Work a second star and then work the two pieces together as below.
Cut a piece of wax cord and tie a double knot in it. Place the two stars wrong sides together and begin crocheting them together, working 1 sc in each st and 3 sc in each point. Lightly stuff and insert the cord as you work.

Cut the cords different lengths so each star hangs at a different height.

assembly

Add beads to the top of each cord if desired and tie the cords around the ring at regular intervals so they hang as desired.

teething ring

Another fun gift to crochet! This is a quick and easy crochet project that gives a fantastic result. The Miffy teething ring is both a beautiful and practical toy for little ones.

* materials

1 ball Durable Coral yarn in 310 White; 1¾oz/50g/137yd/125m
2.5mm (US 1/2, UK 12/13) crochet hook
Fibre filling (for stuffing)
2¾in (70mm) wooden ring

* stitches

ar	adjustable ring
ch	chain
sc	single crochet

Tip: The teething ring is easy to wash. Put it in a laundry bag on a hand wash setting no hotter than 86°F/30°C.

Tip: Over time, wood can start to look dull. You can prevent this by lubricating the wooden part with coconut oil after washing; this is good for the wood and safe for little ones.

ears (make 2)

The ears are worked in continuous rounds. Do not make a chain to start the next round, but simply continue crocheting. Use a stitch marker or a piece of yarn to mark the start of your round.

Round 1: 6 sc into an ar, or work 2 ch, then work 6 sc into the second ch from hook (6 sts).
Round 2: 2 sc in each st (12 sts).
Round 3: 12 sc.
Round 4: *3 sc, 2 sc in next st*, repeat from * to * until the end of this round (15 sts).
Round 5: *4 sc, 2 sc in next st*, repeat from * to * until the end of this row (18 sts).
Rounds 6–13: 18 sc.
Round 14: *4 sc, sc2tog*, repeat from * to * until the end of this round (15 sts).
Rounds 15 and 16: 15 sc.

Fasten off, leaving a long yarn tail for sewing. Stuff the ears.

strip for going round the ring

The strip is worked in rows. Make 1 turning chain at the start of each row. This does not count as a stitch. Work 13 ch.

Row 1: 1 sc in the second ch from hook, 11 sc (12 sts).
Rows 2–20: 1 ch, 12 sc.

Fasten off, leaving a long yarn tail and sew the strip in place on the 2¾in (70mm) ring.

Sew the ears to the strip, with a 2-row gap between them, making sure not to flatten them and keeping their shape intact.

comfort blanket

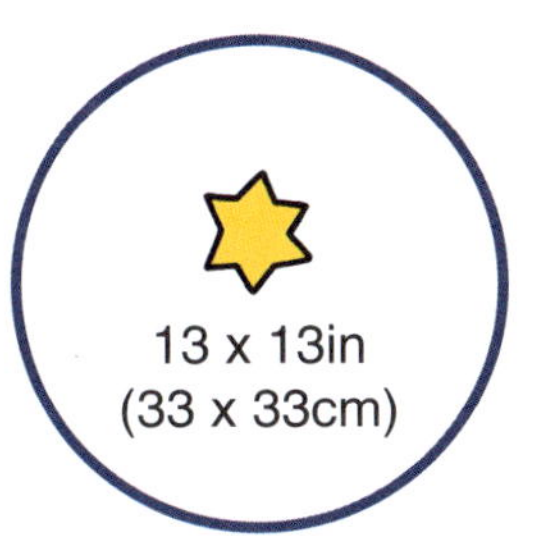

The comfort blanket is made from a granny square and is held tightly in Miffy's hands for a delightful snuggle.
This makes a lovely gift for a newborn or a birthday gift and a wonderful project for the novice crocheter.

★ materials

1 ball of Durable Cosy fine yarn in 310 White (A), 2194 Orange (B) and 2180 Bright Yellow (C); 1¾oz/50g/115yd/105m

1 ball Durable Coral yarn in 310 White (D); 1¾oz/50g/137yd/125m

3.5mm (US 4, UK 9/10) crochet hook

2.5mm (US 1/2, UK 12/13) crochet hook

Fibre filling (for stuffing)

Black thread or embroidery cotton/floss

★ stitches

ar	adjustable ring
ch	chain
dc	double crochet
sc	single crochet
sl st	slip stitch

comfort blanket

The comfort blanket is crocheted using a 3.5mm (US 4, UK 9/10) crochet hook and Durable Cosy fine yarn.
Work a granny square with 15 rounds.
Pattern:
2 rounds in yarn A
2 rounds in yarn C
1 round in yarn B
Repeat twice more until you have a total of 15 rounds.

Round 1: work into an ar, or work 2 ch, then work into the second chain from hook: 3 ch, then work 2 dc into the ring, 2 ch, then *3 dc into the ring, 2 ch*, repeat from * to * twice, end with a sl st in the third chain (4 groups of 3 dc).

Work a sl st in the first dc, and a sl st in the second dc.

Round 2: 3 ch, (2 dc, 2 ch, 3 dc) in the same chain space (first corner made), *(3 dc, 2 ch, 3 dc) in the next chain space*, repeat from * to * twice more, finish with a sl st in the third chain (4 corners made).

Fasten off.

Now join yarn C in the corner space.

Round 3: 3 ch, (2 dc, 2 ch, 3 dc) in the corner space, *3 dc between the clusters of the previous round, (3 dc, 2 ch, 3 dc) in the corner space*, repeat from * to * twice more, 3 dc between the clusters of the previous round, finish with a sl st in the third chain.

Work a sl st in the second dc and a sl st in the third dc.

Round 4: 3 ch, (2 dc, 2 ch, 3 dc) in the next chain space (= space in the corner), *3 dc between each cluster of the previous row, (3 dc, 2 ch, 3 dc) in the space in the corner*, repeat from * to * twice more, 3 dc between each cluster of the previous round, finish with a sl st in the third chain.

Fasten off and change to yarn B.

Repeat round 4 until you have a total of 15 rounds.

The ears, head and arms are worked in continuous rounds. Do not make a chain to start the next round, but simply continue crocheting. Use a stitch marker or a piece of yarn to mark the start of your round.

ears (make 2)

Round 1: using 2.5mm (US 1/2, UK 12/13) hook and yarn D, work 6 sc into an ar, or work 2 ch, then work 6 sc into the second ch from hook (6 sts).
Round 2: 2 sc in each st (12 sts).
Round 3: 12 sc.
Round 4: *3 sc, 2 sc in next st*, repeat from * to * until the end of this round (15 sts).
Round 5: *4 sc, 2 sc in next st*, repeat from * to * until the end of this round (18 sts).
Rounds 6–13: 18 sc.
Round 14: *4 sc, sc2tog*, repeat from * to * to end of round (15 sts).
Rounds 15 and 16: 15 sc.

Fasten off and work a second ear. The second ear is not fastened off.

Take the first ear and continue crocheting into the stitch next to the last st of round 16. Continue to round 1 to make the head.

head

Round 1: 2 sc, 2 sc in the next st, *4 sc, 2 sc in the next st*, repeat from * to * across both ears and end with 2 sc (36 sts).
Round 2: *5 sc, 2 sc in next st*, repeat from * to * until the end of this round (42 sts).
Round 3: 7 sc, *1 sc, 2 sc in the next st*, repeat from * to * twice more, 15 sc, *1 sc, 2 sc in the next st*, repeat from * to * twice more, 8 sc (48 sts).
Rounds 4 and 5: 48 sc.
Round 6: 9 sc, *1 sc, 2 sc in next st*, repeat from * to * twice more, 18 sc, *1 sc, 2 sc in next st*, repeat from * to * twice more, 9 sc (54 sts).
Round 7: 54 sc.
Round 8: *8 sc, 2 sc in next st*, repeat from * to * until the end of this round (60 sts).
Rounds 9–14: 60 sc.
Round 15: *8 sc, sc2tog*, repeat from * to * to end of this row (54 sts).
Round 16: 54 sc.
Round 17: *7 sc, sc2tog*, repeat from * to * until the end of this round (48 sts).
Round 18: 48 sc.
Round 19: *6 sc, sc2tog*, repeat from * to * until the end of this row (42 sts).
Round 20: 42 sc.

From here, stuff the ears and head.

Round 21: *5 sc, sc2tog*, repeat from * to * to end of this round (36 sts).
Round 22: *4 sc, sc2tog*, repeat from * to * until the end of this round (30 sts).
Round 23: *3 sc, sc2tog*, repeat from * to * to end of this round (24 sts).
Round 24: *2 sc, sc2tog*, repeat from * to * to end of this round (18 sts).
Round 25: *1 sc, sc2tog*, repeat from * to * until the end of this round (12 sts).
Round 26: *sc2tog*, repeat from * to * to end of this round (6 sts).

Fasten off, close the ring and embroider the eyes and a mouth using black thread or embroidery cotton/floss.

Embroider the eyes between rounds 14 and 16, spaced 9 stitches apart. Stitch the mouth between rounds 18 and 19 and rounds 20 and 21, making sure there is a 4-stitch space in between (see photo).

arms (make 2)

Round 1: 6 sc into an ar, or work 2 ch, then work 6 sc into the second ch from hook (6 sts).
Round 2: 2 sc in each st (12 sts).
Round 3: *3 sc, 2 sc in next st*, repeat from * to * until the end of this round (15 sts).
Round 4: *4 sc, 2 sc in next st*, repeat from * to * until the end of this round (18 sts).
Rounds 5–20: 18 sc.

Lightly stuff the lower part of the arm and sew the arms in place under the head. Wrap Miffy's arms around the crocheted granny blanket and sew it in place.

blanket

This Miffy blanket is crocheted using the corner to corner technique and consists of 9 squares. The 9 squares combine to form a wonderfully large blanket you can snuggle under. You can also choose 6 or 4 squares, and mix and match the pattern yourself. A pattern with possibilities galore!

★ size

The entire blanket, consisting of 9 squares, is 42½in (108cm) wide and 61½in (156cm) long. Each square is 14¼in (36cm) wide and 20½in (52cm) long.

★ materials

10 balls of Durable Cosy fine yarn in 310 White (A), 16 balls in 2194 Orange (B), 3 balls in 2106 Peacock Blue (C), 3 balls in 2152 Leaf Green (D), 4 balls in 2180 Bright Yellow (E) and 3 balls in 325 Black (F); 1¾oz/50g/115yd/105m

3.5mm (US 4, UK 9/10) crochet hook

★ stitches

ch chain

dc double crochet

hdc half double crochet

sl st slip stitch

The panels are crocheted together with slip stitches using Durable Cosy fine yarn in 310 White.

Tip: Follow along with the corner to corner steps as you crochet.

corner to corner technique

The corner to corner technique was used for this blanket. This technique is perfect for pixel crochet, allowing you to incorporate images directly into your blanket design. This form of crochet seems challenging but is quite straightforward once you know what to do. Here we break it down into easy-to-follow steps.

Corner to corner crochet is literally crocheting from one corner to another. In doing so, we start in the bottom right corner and work towards the top left corner. The stitches used here – chains and double crochet stitches – form a cluster that ultimately represents a single pixel.

Read the text step by step and go through the pattern carefully.

Step 1: 6 ch, then work 1 dc in the fourth ch from hook, 1 dc in the fifth ch and the last dc in the last (sixth) chain.
This is your first cluster.
Now you will increase.

Step 2: 6 ch, then work 1 dc in the fourth ch from hook, 1 dc in the fifth ch and the last dc in the last (sixth) chain.

Now turn this cluster towards the first cluster and make a sl st in the chain space of the first cluster.

Next work 3 ch and then 3 dc around the chain space. That is then your second cluster.

Step 3: 6 ch, then work 1 dc in the fourth ch from hook, 1 dc in the fifth ch and the last dc in the last (sixth) chain.

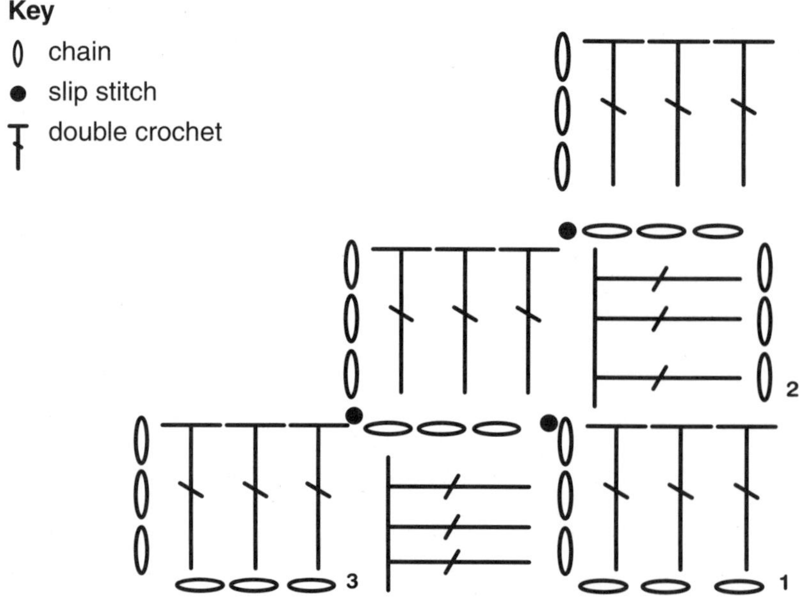

1
2
3

1
2

Now turn this cluster towards the previous cluster and make a sl st in the chain space of the previous cluster.

Now 3 ch and 3 dc around the chain space. That is then your next cluster.

To change colour, switch as soon as you crochet a slip stitch to join your next cluster. This can be done in the same way you normally change colours. You can choose to carry the yarn up, so that you have to fasten off as little as possible.

Decreasing using the corner to corner technique:

Step 1: turn your work and crochet 4 sl st (3 in the dc and 1 in the chain space). Now 3 ch and then 3 dc around the chain space. Make a sl st to the next cluster and make new clusters again until the end. End with a sl st in the chain space.

Step 2: now turn your work and again crochet 4 sl st (3 in the dc and 1 in the chain space). Then work another 3 ch and work another 3 dc around the chain space of the previous cluster.

Repeat the process for each block until they are all complete.

crocheting together

All blocks are joined together with yarn A. Place the 9 blocks in the desired pattern on the table, with the correct side facing down. Work 2 blocks together and then attach the next one, to form a row of 3. In the same way, crochet the rest of the blocks together.

crocheting the blocks together

Hold 2 blocks wrong sides together. Join yarn A to the top corner of the first block. Chain 2 (counts as first hdc), work 1 hdc in the second block. Then work another 1 hdc in the next stitch of the first block, and 1 hdc in the next stitch of the second block. Continue in this way, working 1 hdc alternately in the first and second block up to the next corner.

Fasten off and weave in the yarn end. Crochet the third block to the second. Make 3 rows of 3 blocks and crochet the rows together. Fasten off and weave in the yarn end.

border around the blanket

Using yarn A, crochet a border of dc in each stitch, with 2 dc in the chain space at the corners. Start in one of the corners. 3 ch (counts as first dc), 1 dc in each subsequent stitch. End the round with 1 sl st in the uppermost chain of the 3 turning chains.

Fasten off and weave in the yarn end.

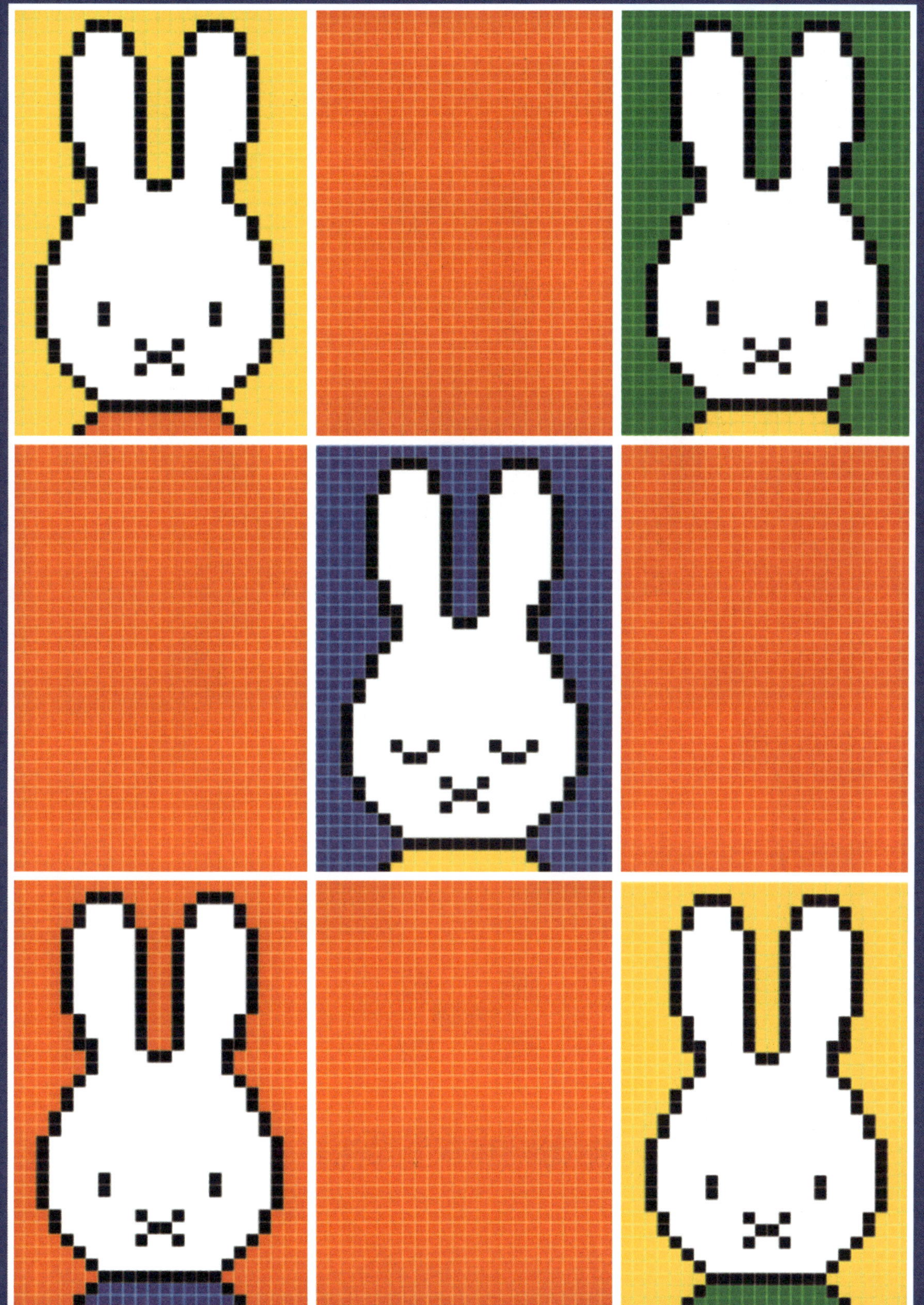

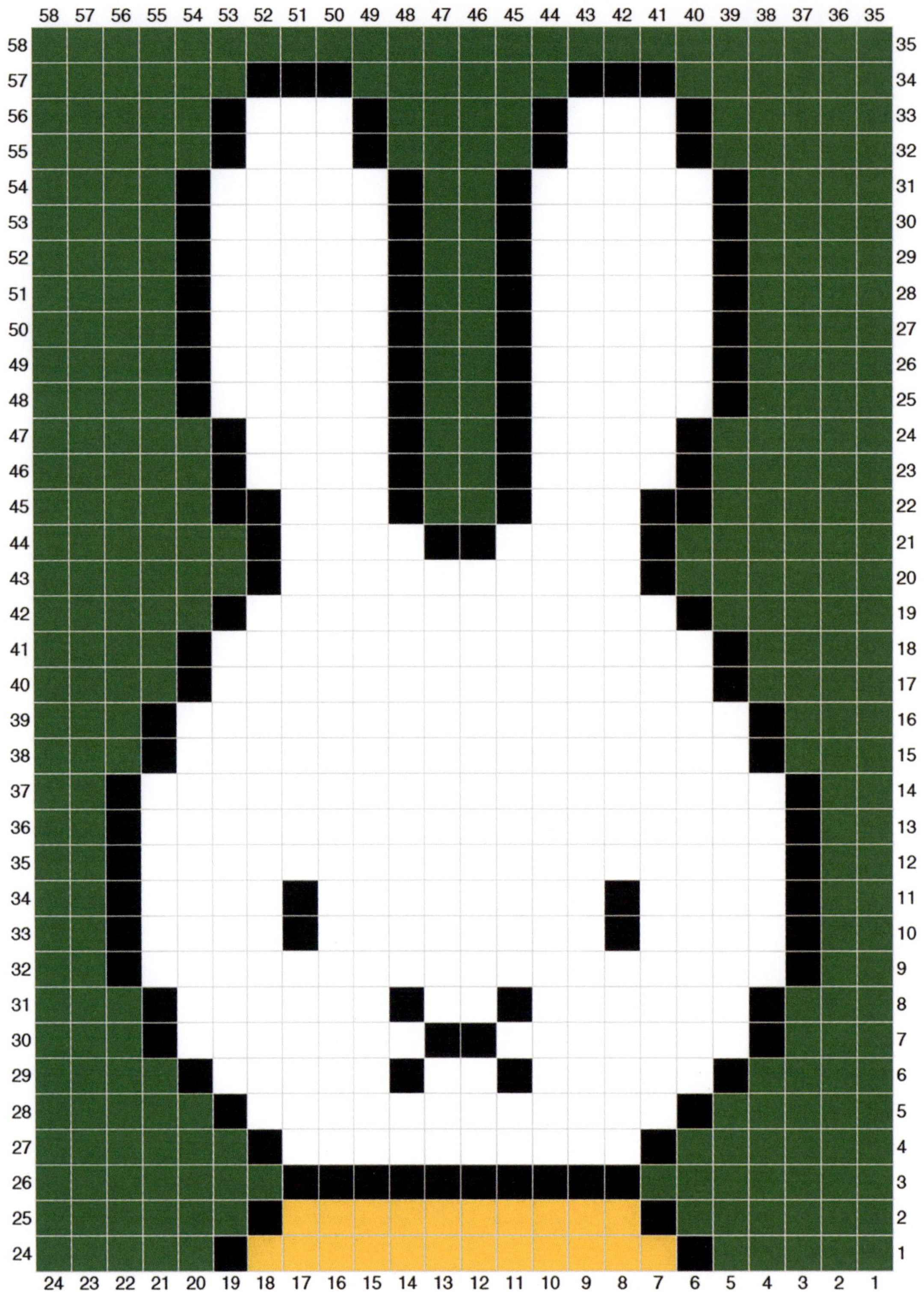

58 57 56 55 54 53 52 51 50 49 48 47 46 45 44 43 42 41 40 39 38 37 36 35
58 57 56 55 54 53 52 51 50 49 48 47 46 45 44 43 42 41 40 39 38 37 36 35 34 33 32 31 30 29 28 27 26 25 24
35 34 33 32 31 30 29 28 27 26 25 24 23 22 21 20 19 18 17 16 15 14 13 12 11 10 9 8 7 6 5 4 3 2 1
24 23 22 21 20 19 18 17 16 15 14 13 12 11 10 9 8 7 6 5 4 3 2 1

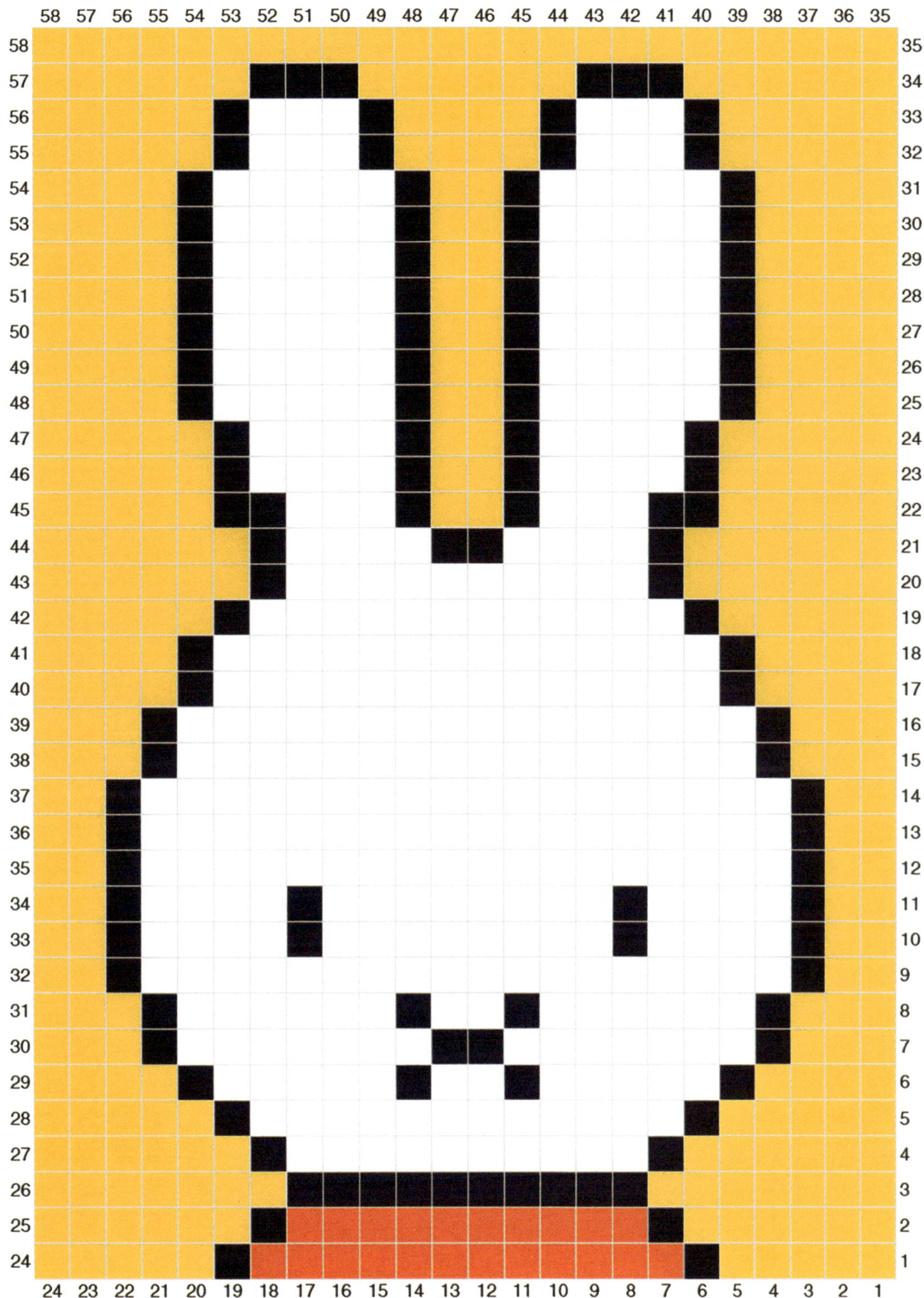

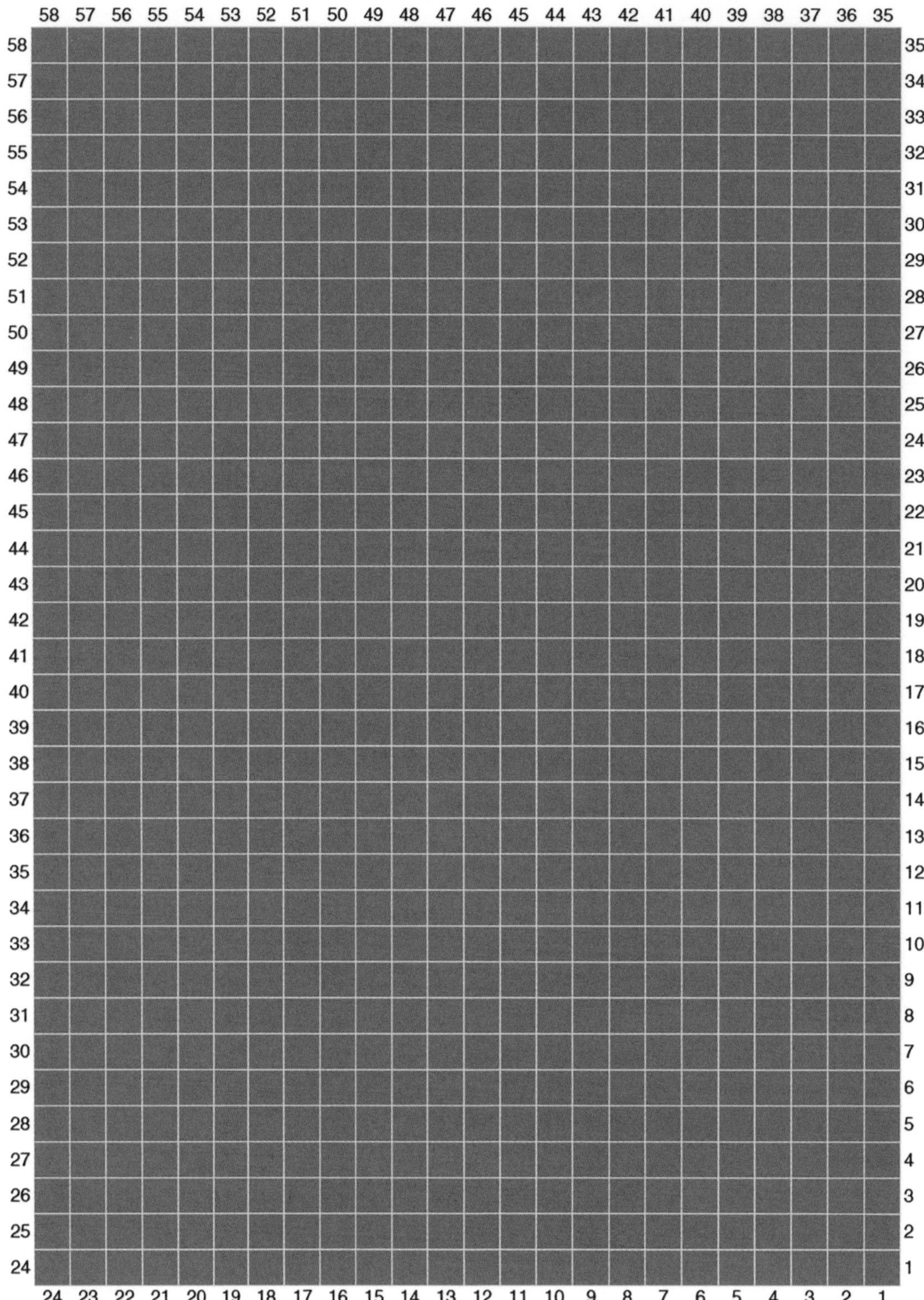

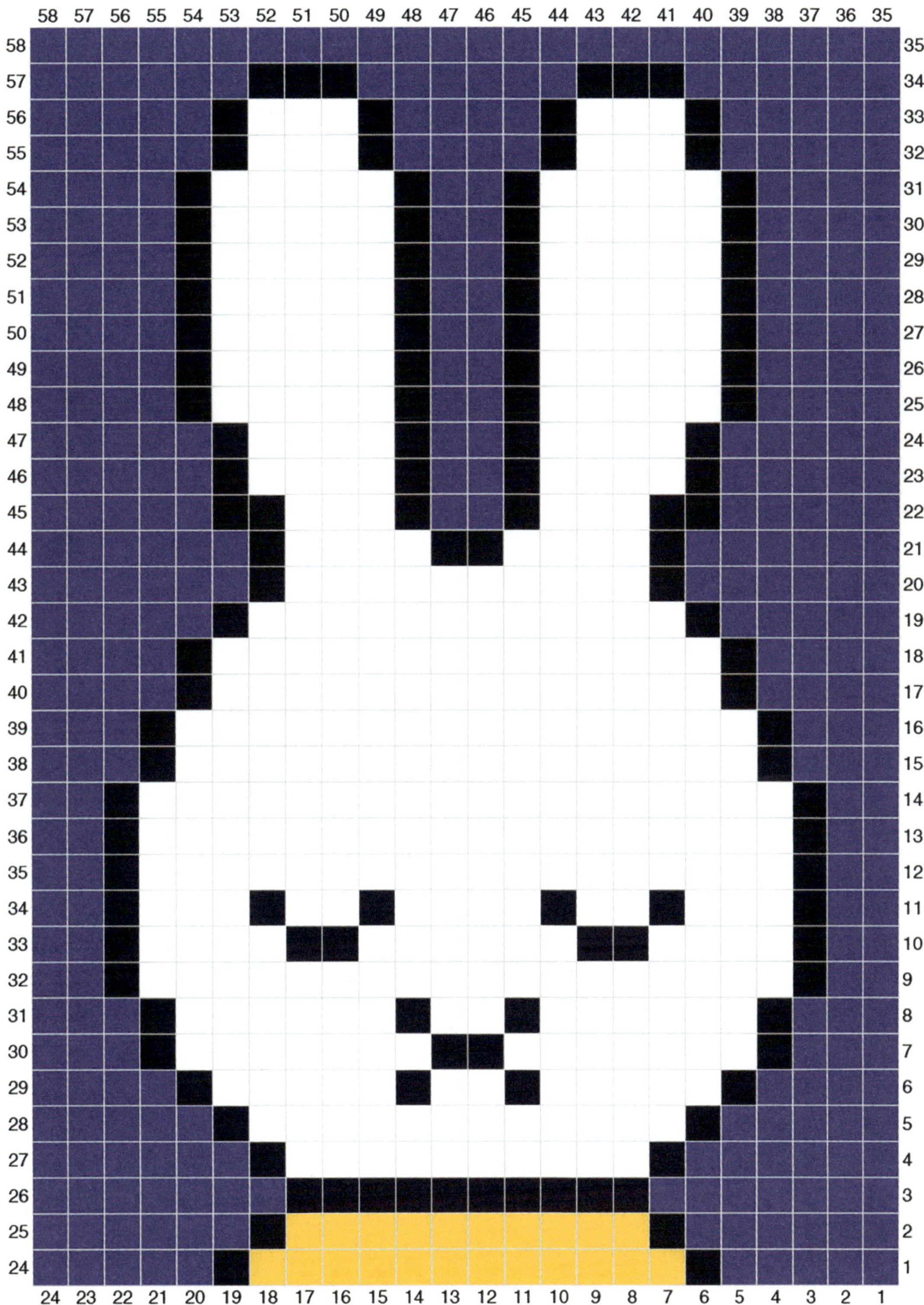
58 57 56 55 54 53 52 51 50 49 48 47 46 45 44 43 42 41 40 39 38 37 36 35
24 23 22 21 20 19 18 17 16 15 14 13 12 11 10 9 8 7 6 5 4 3 2 1

pillow

Incorporate Miffy into your soft furnishings with this pretty crocheted pillow. The corner to corner technique is used for this project. The example is crocheted using white yarn, but you can of course choose any colour to suit your interior.

★ materials

5 balls of Durable Cosy fine yarn in 310 White (A) and 1 ball in 325 Black (B); 1¾oz/50g/115yd/105m
3.5mm (US 4, UK 9/10) crochet hook
Pillow insert 19¾ x 19¾in (50 x 50cm)

★ stitches

dc	double crochet
hdc	half double crochet
sc	single crochet
sl st	slip stitch

Tip: Follow along with the corner to corner technique steps as you crochet.

corner to corner crocheting

The corner to corner technique is used for the pillow. This technique is perfect for pixel crochet, allowing you to incorporate images directly into your blanket design. This form of crochet seems challenging, but is quite straightforward once you know what to do. Here we break it down into easy-to-follow steps.

Corner to corner crocheting is literally crocheting from one corner to another. With this technique, you start in the bottom right corner and work towards the top left corner. The stitches we work here, chains and double crochet stitches, form a cluster and ultimately represent one pixel.

Read the text step by step and go through the pattern carefully.

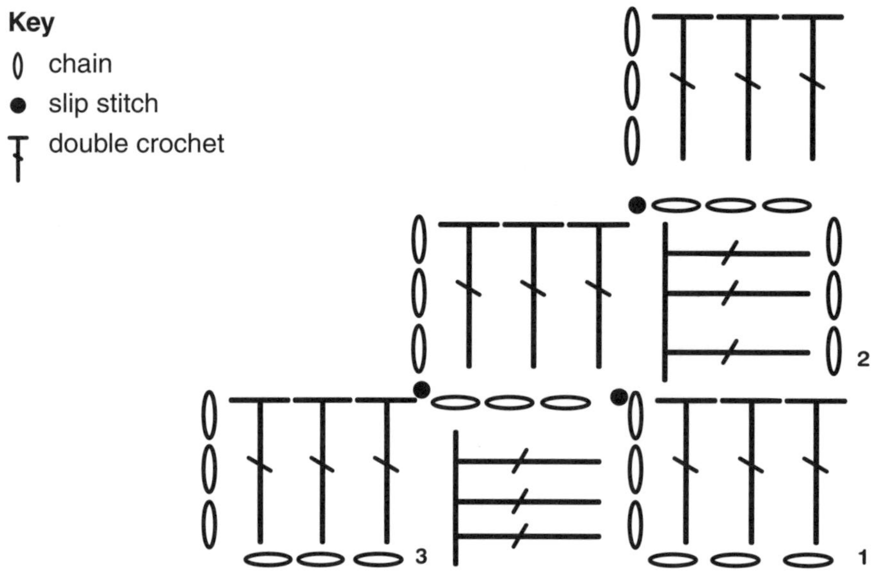

Step 1: 6 ch, then work 1 dc in the fourth ch from hook, 1 dc in the fifth ch and the last dc in the last (sixth) ch.

This is your first cluster. Now begin to increase.

Step 2: 6 ch, then work 1 dc in the fourth ch from hook, 1 dc in the fifth ch and the last dc in the last (sixth) ch.

Now turn the cluster towards the first cluster, then make a sl st in the chain space of the first cluster.

3 ch, then work 3 dc in the chain space. That is then your second cluster.

Step 3: 6 ch, then work 1 dc in the fourth ch from hook, 1 dc in the fifth ch and the last dc in the last (sixth) ch.

Now turn this cluster towards the previous cluster and make a sl st in the chain space of the previous cluster.

Now work 3 ch and work 3 dc around the chain space. This is your next cluster.

The colour change goes as follows: as soon as you crochet a sl st to make your next cluster, switch colours. Do this the same way you usually change colours. You can choose to carry the yarn up, so that you have to fasten off as little as possible.

Decreasing using the corner to corner technique:

Step 1: turn your work and work 4 sl st (3 in the dc and 1 in the chain space). Now work 3 ch, then work 3 dc in the chain space. Make a sl st to the next cluster and continue making new clusters until the end. End with a sl st in the chain space.

Step 2: now turn your work and again crochet 4 sl st (3 in the dc and 1 in the chain space). Then work another 3 ch and 3 dc around the chain space of the previous cluster.

Repeat this until you have crocheted both blocks.

joining the pillow together

Place the front and back on top of each other, with the right sides facing out. Start in one of the corners. Join yarn A to the corner chain space on the front. Chain 2 (counts as first hdc), then work 1 hdc into the chain space of the same corner on the back piece. Then work another 1 hdc in the front, and 1 hdc in the back. Continue in this way, working 1 hdc in each stitch between the corners, alternating between the front and back of the pillow, to the next corner. Join 3 sides together and then tuck in the pillow insert. Join the last side together as before, working 1 hdc through both layers. Fasten off and weave in the yarn end.

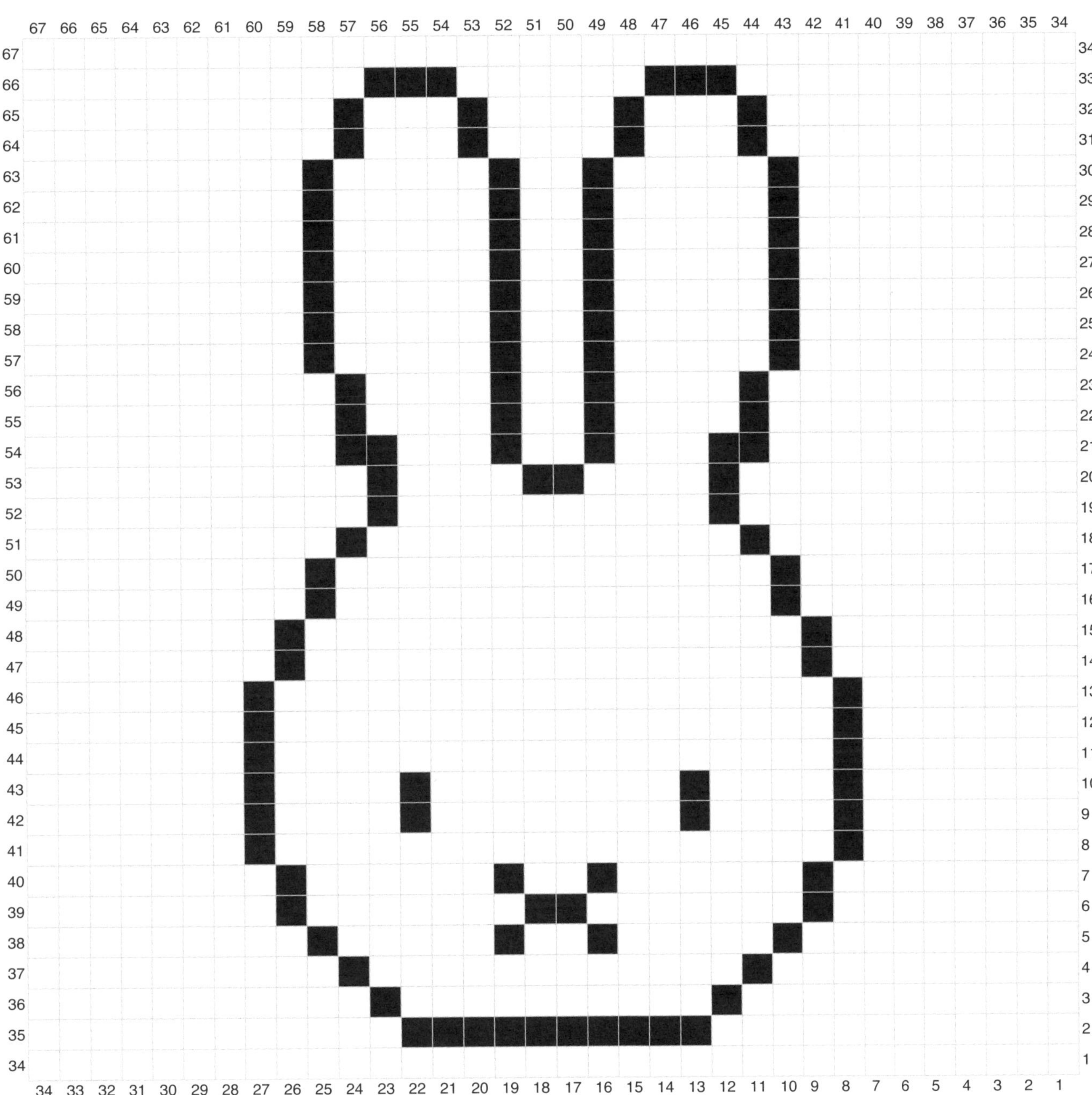

acknowledgements

I look back on the adventure of creating this book with great gratitude. This project was a journey full of challenges, inspiration and teamwork, and I would like to express my sincere thanks to the people who made it possible.

A special thanks goes to Marike den Brok, my publisher, for her invaluable support, her incredible cooperation and the unconditional trust she had in me throughout this process.

Desk editor Heleen Onstenk also deserves a special mention for her help in editing the text. If I ever stumbled over my words, she was always there to support me, and I'm incredibly grateful for that.

Josephine van Bennekom and Femke den Hertog have perfectly captured the unique Miffy atmosphere with their beautiful design – hats off to them!

Ronald R. Reinders has used his stunning photography to bring the crochet creations to life on the pages of this book; they are a joy to look at.

A word of thanks also goes to Remco Brouwer and his team, who supported us with their Durable brand and other materials.

Thanks to the meticulous testing by my test crocheters, the crochet patterns in this book are of the highest quality. Dear girls, by now you are more than just my crochet testers; you have become my friends! Annemieke van Dijk, Elsbeth-Nynke Bos, Famke in den Bosch, Tessa Janssen, Linda in den Bosch-van Dam, Anne van Duimen, Irene Bos, thank you!

A big thank you to Marijke van Oord for (test) crocheting the blanket – that was no small task!

My family deserves credit for their patience and unconditional support throughout this adventure. Dear Marinus, Justin Liam and Roan James, big hugs to you.

Last but not least, thanks to you, the readers, for embracing this book. Without your enthusiasm, this book would not have been such a success.

This was an amazing adventure that I look back on with enormous pleasure and pride. Crocheting for a big brand that holds a special place in people's hearts isn't always easy, but together we've created something truly extraordinary.

With warm greetings,
Kimberley Zwaans